ADVAN

"In *One October Night*, Leo McCarthy has taken any father's worst nightmare and turned it into pure love in his community while celebrating the life of his daughter. It's amazing what he's accomplished with Mariah's Challenge. I'm proud to call Leo a friend and a staple of the Butte community."
— *Tim Montana, major-label recording artist and hit songwriter*

"How do you articulate what a fourteen-year-old daughter means to a family? How do you describe what a dimple-faced child who loves bowling adds to a family's collective heart? How do you live through losing her forever because of a murderer behind the wheel of a truck? The struggle for the survivors is one that no one wants to live through. No training can prepare you. My dear friend Leo McCarthy tells us this beautifully while demonstrating that tragedy can be a source of strength. Through pain and catastrophe, we can help our children and our future. I accept Mariah's Challenge."
—*Rob O'Neill, motivational speaker, Fox News contributor, and former United States Navy SEAL*

"Leo McCarthy takes you on an emotional journey through every parent's nightmare, the loss of a child. In *One October Night*, he takes a loss that shattered his family and shows how to create something positive from pain and anger. In this book, you will see how a tragedy in the former mining camp of Butte inspired Mariah's Challenge, a movement to change the culture of underage drinking and driving. Be prepared to have your heart melted and your eyes flooded by this emotional story of anguish and strength."
— *Ron Davis, owner, Butte Broadcasting (KBOW)*

"I was with Mariah the night of the tragedy. Being one of the last faces she saw before she moved on from this world has made me feel that Mariah has always been there as my guardian angel. 'Spirit in the Sky' by Norman Greenbaum was played at her funeral, and I listen to this song before every competition knowing my guardian angel is with me.

"Leo's book shines light on how powerful a community can be. Mariah is now with all of us, affecting the decisions we make and influencing us to be responsible people. Leo also shines light on the flaws of our culture. Laws not being enforced and people continuing to drink and drive. It is sad to know that a lot of these people are set up for failure. The culture and habits of these communities make it very hard to make the conscious decision not to get behind the wheel. This tragedy will always be a major part of my life. But it will never be reversed.

"After reading *One October Night* I am now inspired to do what I can to change the culture and habits that lead to these tragedies."
— *Brad Wilson, American freestyle skier, competitor in 2014 Winter Olympics*

ONE OCTOBER NIGHT

a memoir

LEO MCCARTHY

The information, views, and opinions expressed in this book are solely those of the author and they reflect his best recollection of the events reported herein or are based on notes and materials created at the time.

ISBN: 971-1-59152-300-0
© 2021 by Leo McCarthy

All photos courtesy of the McCarthy Family
Book design by Steph Lehmann

All rights reserved. This book may not be reproduced in whole or in part by any means (with the exception of short quotes for the purpose of review) without the permission of the publisher.

For more information or to order extra copies of this book call
Farcountry Press toll free at (800) 821-3874 or visit www.farcountrypress.com

sweetgrassbooks
an imprint of Farcountry Press

Produced by Sweetgrass Books
PO Box 5630, Helena, MT 59604; (800) 821-3874; www.sweetgrassbook.com

Published by the Mariah Daye McCarthy Scholarship Foundation.

The views expressed by the author/publisher in this book do not necessarily represent the views of, nor should they be attributed to, Sweetgrass Books. Sweetgrass books is not responsible for the author/publisher's work.

Produced and printed in the United States of America.

25 24 23 22 21   1 2 3 4 5

Contents

Foreword by Linda Piccolo vi

Part One

1 Home 3
2 Innocence 17
3 Game Day 22
4 The Voicemail 27
5 Bedside 31
6 We Got Him 38
7 Last Rites 45
8 Missoula 49
9 Rocky Waves 54
10 Public Mourning 59

Part Two

11 Crime and Consequences 67
12 The Birth of Mariah's Challenge 74
13 Hitting the Road 78
14 Loss, Pain, and Gratitude 93
15 Fréamhacha Agus Brainsí 99
Epilogue 106

Additional Materials

Victim Impact Statement of Leo McCarthy 111
Excerpts from Mariah's Challenge, a play by Linda Piccolo 125
"Tap 'er Light: The best we all can be,"
    by Bill Foley, from *The Montana Standard* 141
"21 Butte Seniors Honored at 10th Annual
    Mariah's Challenge Scholarship Ceremony,"
    by Maddie Vincent, from *The Montana Standard* 145
Thanks & Acknowledgments 147
A Prayer in Closing 151
About the Author 152

Foreword

I had been teaching English and Theatre for seventeen years at Jefferson High School in the small town of Boulder, just thirty miles from Butte. As yearbook advisor, each fall I took my staff to Butte to solicit ads. Invariably, Butte native and insurance agent Leo McCarthy was kind and attentive to each student, asking their ages and interests. And he always purchased an ad. His was one of our first stops, and although they were short meetings and only once a year, I found myself drawn to his jovial, caring personality.

Nothing could be more horrible for the McCarthys and two other families than the violent and brutal incident that took place on the snowy night of October 27, 2007. It was while reading *The Montana Standard* in the faculty room during my break that I learned the first crushing details. I started weeping. As the parent of two children and having a strong relationship with the 135 teens I interacted with each day, I knew that Mariah McCarthy, Kaitlyn Okrusch, and Valarie Kilmer could have been my own children, or my students.

The story of this crime stayed in the papers and would not shake from my consciousness. As well, having met Leo, I felt a particular bond with the McCarthys. Then, sometime around New Year's Eve, I had an epiphany. This was more than news, this was tragedy. Not just for the families involved, but for all of Butte and Montana.

As an actress, director, and playwright, I knew the power of theatre not only to tell a story but to release the emotions of such an enormous event, and after much thought I took the leap to interject my small skill to try to bring some catharsis to my community, and to the actors and students. The ancient Greeks called it Katharsis. Aristotle believed it was the necessary purification of emotions through art that resulted in renewal and restoration. The night and lifelong aftermath of October 27, 2007, called for just that in order to honor Mariah, Kaitlyn, and Valarie, and to move an audience in a positive way.

To bring this tragedy to the stage, I continued to follow the crime in print. But feeling the need to expose myself in a more immediate way to the human drama being played out in public, I took personal leave to attend the trial. In doing so, I met Janice and Jenna and the Okrusches and Kilmers. Leo and Janice not only granted me permission to write the play and interview the participants but also graciously allowed me complete access to Mariah's room, sharing copies of her journal and poetry. Later they gave this same access to my high school actresses playing Jenna and Janice. They also arranged for me to interview Valarie and Peggy Kilmer and Kaitlyn and Margi Okrusch, families united by tragedy, whose pain was deeply personal, yet universal. (A year later four teenaged girls were struck on a road near Missoula. Two died. The driver was drunk.)

In particular, my interview with Shane Ford left me shaken. Here was a man relaxing at home on a Saturday night. He received an urgent call to return to his business and took an unusual route home, bringing him into the path of the driver moments after he had struck the three girls. Shane questioned him and heard the story of a struck deer. Instead of driving home, he was compelled to look for the animal. He found three dying girls. Shane called for help, and his wife and son arrived at the scene and offered emotional support to the two injured girls as Shane applied CPR to Mariah until the EMTs took over. His intercession saved the lives of Kaitlyn and Valarie and kept Mariah alive as her parents raced to the hospital. His actions that night were not a coincidence, they were divine intervention. He became the biblical Good Samaritan. He manifested good out of evil.

As a result of their great loss, the McCarthys could have become recluses in their home, drowning in their grief. But they did not, and that is what makes their story unique. They refused to let Mariah become just another white cross on the side of a Montana road. And Leo found the mettle to crawl out of the pit of despair to create something life-affirming from the devastation and death a drunk driver left behind.

It is a testament to the people of Butte that they embraced the "Challenge," standing up to bullying and the entitlement of teen drinking and collectively saying, "No more." That first year thirty-one local teens took the Challenge. All told, going on four hundred scholarships have been awarded to college-bound youth who refuse to bow to peer pressure, and who hold themselves to a higher standard.

Leo has worked tirelessly to promote the program, near and far. He and Jimm continue to speak out about the dangers of underage drinking. Now, a husband and father who views himself as the unlikeliest of authors has told his story. I cannot imagine the courage and perseverance it took to write this powerful book. On top of the resilience it takes to repeatedly open those wounds and relive that awful night in front of audiences of strangers. May Mariah Daye McCarthy live forever as a darling, effervescent fourteen-year-old who loved her Irish heritage and her Butte roots, who cherished her family and friends and spoke to angels. No longer a victim of darkness, but a catalyst to light, she is now truly an angel.

—*Linda Piccolo, April 2021* ❖

PART ONE

*C*old early morning air is often still in the mountains, more so in autumn when the coolness, having settled in the valleys for its nightly slumber among the saw-toothed ridgelines, can now awaken into a new day. The sky is clear, and a hint of paleness in the south allows the edges of the many cloud wisps to sharpen into focus. These clouds always make me think of God's paintbrush strokes, so airy and delicate, resting adjacent to heaven's gate. But it is not quite dawn yet, and the sun has not awoken to burn off the chill. On mornings like these, a patina of frost blankets the leaves, green lawns, mine trucks, and delicately carved pumpkins sitting on the wobbly, weather-beaten porches of the glorious mining town of Butte, Montana.

 I know there are people awake this time of day, even on a Saturday, but not many. It is an innocent time, when the stillness evokes sanctuary and all the world is goodness. Some are trying to sleep late, while others catch up on the week's deprivation, and the early risers haven't yet reached the ignitions of their oversized Ford or Chevy trucks to melt Jack Frost's frozen fingerprints off their cracked windshields. ◈

1

HOME

She had a way of being Mariah. I miss her not being with her lovely sister Jenna. The two, inseparable as young gals, were so good to each other. Sibling conflict more severe than a mean look seldom erupted. I hope and wish Mariah speaks to Jenna in dreams and in the quietness of the night.

The McCarthy household stirred and stumbled. We have a modest two-story home with tan siding, considered fairly new for this area, located toward the end of a cul-de-sac on a quiet street, and the only real passersby are neighbors. Montana autumns are overly dry, which slows lawn growth almost entirely. Ours had not been cut in weeks. If it weren't for the sprinkler heads dotting the green perimeter, our rectangle of property would have been crispy brown on that October morning.

We are in a sweet spot, away from the brick and mortar that makes up Butte's historical Uptown and the residential neighborhoods there, but not far enough out to live among the picturesque sprawl of cattle-dotted rolling hills in the shadow of the majestic snowcapped Highland Mountains to the south. Aside from a modest Harrison Avenue "strip" with a handful of recognizable box stores and traffic lights, at a population of around 34,000 Butte has been relatively immune to the development seen in other towns. Nor are there any suburbs.

What we have on Blacktail Lane is an elegant mix of proximity to the bustle of downtown and an atmosphere of solitude and space. Truly an American Dream: a place where Janice, my wife, and our two incredible daughters, Jenna and Mariah, created the life I once hoped I could provide them. A place to make and share a foundation of lifetime memories. On our street I have always felt the perfect blend of slowness and stillness.

One of life's pleasures in Butte has been taking my girls to see the Orediggers play football in the fall. On this Saturday, the Orediggers would square off against the Montana Western Bulldogs. For longer than I can remember, I have been a member of the Touchdown Club and an avid supporter of Tech athletics.

Montana Tech is located on the flanks of Big Butte, a landmark on the western edge of town. Founded in 1889, just eleven years after our state joined the union, as the Montana School of Mines, the four-year institution occupies a vantage point that makes it feel like a protector watching over Butte. Originally a single structure, Main Hall, the campus has a distinctive ornamental red-brick style seen in many buildings dating from the turn of the previous century. Now part of the University of Montana system, with trademark modesty some around town call it "Harvard on the Hill."

Yes, Montana Tech provides a world-class education (it is on the leading edge in mining, petroleum, geology, and environmental engineering) in a distinctive landscape, but it also turns green-behind-the-ears kids into contributing, grounded citizens. Thanks to the HPER Complex and improvements to Bob Green Field at historic Alumni Coliseum, the sports facilities are on par with those in much larger schools. (We've come a long way since competitive quoits—a game in which players pitch flat rings of iron or rope at a stake.) Putting on the Tech-green jersey may mean that game time is soon, but those colors stand for much more, and the appropriately named Orediggers have bolstered Butte's exposure near and far.

Something about the Diggers is in my blood. Although I never played football at Tech, I was somewhat part of the history through my dad, Dan McCarthy, who dedicated seventeen years to the team. I was one of the many "coach's kids" who grew up around Alumni Coliseum. Perhaps the camaraderie is what I gravitate toward; after an all-night pig roast (which I have helped prepare, though never actually endured), a tailgating party comes with its share of stories. Stories of stupid college days and of men on the football battlefield, reminiscing about girls and school. The edges are always blurred by jostling bullshit of the very best kind.

Perhaps, too, it is what the arena of sports at its best provides that I cherish. All those intangible life lessons that cannot be taught in textbooks: hard work, sacrifice, leadership and followership, working as a team for a common goal, winning and losing with grace. Those qualities of integrity never sufficiently approached or acted upon.

Like many Butte kids, then and now, I played football from the elementary flag on to junior high and high school. Not a star or standout, just a team member. The lessons from coaches, teammates, and fans helped me create mature actions and behavior. Sound decisions made in the heat of a fourth quarter homecoming game prepared me for challenges in the grind of daily life. Learning how to accept losing a city championship, how to respond and improve your strength and conditioning, how to defend a teammate, and how to carry yourself with class and dignity under duress all create character.

Running around the house in the rush of preparation for an Orediggers tailgate party never fails to stir memories, mostly of Jenna and Mariah helping me cook and serve burgers or brats during the pregame festivities. Eventually, and every father knows this is inevitable, Jenna found new interests, taking her away from the grill and smoke, but Mariah always stuck around with her dad. My cohort served up the finest in tailgating barbeque cuisine.

That time always felt special, but I did not know that she had so much fun until I read some of her journals. Those mornings have taken on more significance now, and I am thankful for all of her and Jenna's little graces, graces that appear with force waves of emotion that cascade over me, ragged as they come, smoother as they leave.

October 27, 2007, started like any pregame Saturday, with Janice preparing breakfast for the girls, who both slept in late, not an uncommon occurrence after a long week of school. The recent summer days of carefree fun had, as usual, slipped into anxious autumn dreams of class schedules, homework, and time with friends.

We all have visions for our children. I think every father, somewhere in his depths, sees himself playing catch with his son in the front yard, or teaching him the mechanics of a jump shot in the illumination from the porch light as the sun goes down over the driveway. Such visions are understandable, but when it comes down to it, a parent simply wants healthy, happy children. Period. On this day, Janice and I are blessed with two daughters, who stole every ounce of my heart when they came into this world. A father could not ask for more. He cheers just as loud when his girl completes a dance routine as when his son scores a touchdown. Our Mariah is drawn to sports as much as any boy could be, and plays basketball and volleyball. When either of my daughters excels in a competitive activity, whether it's tee-ball, dance, or bowling, you can find me fired up, yelling harder and harder, and when they come up short, I hug them more deeply still. It is participation in their lives that counts, not the reliving of your own past through them.

Jenna has been full of excitement and wonder since she was born. She embraced the role of cruise director and source of information to her little sister. They loved to perform plays and dance skits together for all who were lucky to see them. Jenna's patience and big-sister love, her being a role model, will always stay with me. Jenna knew the parameters and rules and was adept in showing how to get around some of the less serious ones, and Mariah was eager to follow in her sister's steps. Though our sweet Jenna certainly felt both sides of being the first-born, she thrived in that role and our family is far stronger because of her. She may have taught us as much as we taught her.

Mariah I would describe as a tenaciously hard worker. This innate quality helped her overcome being cursed with my intelligence rather than blessed with

Janice's. Some subjects didn't come easy right away, but with practice and sweat she was rewarded with a 3.68 grade point average until her freshman year.

She never quit anything. When I helped her prepare for so many of her tests, I would use concrete stories and objects to help her grasp abstract ideas. Mariah was a constant reader, mostly science fiction along with some human-relationship stories. School was a testing ground, and when she was not satisfied, diligence and drive inevitably kicked in. This is a tribute to her character, even as she was surrounded by the many distractions in a world of manic multi-tasking where the newest, shiniest bauble gets all of the current generation's attention. I envied that aspect of her personality.

Mariah's hobbies were varied. She wrote in journals that now serve as an insight into her quiet self and the depth of her individuality. She also enjoyed drawing, and especially drawing angels. A proud father, I must say that as a fifth grader at Hillcrest Elementary she was awarded first prize in a competition sponsored by NorthWestern Energy. She lit up when we saw her entry on the Montana Street billboard; the same drawing was distributed throughout the state. During sixth grade, a picture she submitted to the annual Christmas Stroll was chosen to appear on all the fundraising buttons sold that year. Both award-winning pictures included angels.

When it came to athletics, Mariah mirrored her toughness in the classroom. She was a bowler from fourth grade on, enjoying the atmosphere of friendship. Bowling requires finesse and skill, and she had both: her average was 205! She also played basketball until seventh grade and continued on with volleyball. She did not make the freshman team, but in true Mariah form was adamant about sharpening her skills and trying out the next year. She played spring volleyball for the U-14 league, which traveled throughout Montana and Utah. She was planning to play tennis in her freshman year, and to try her patience at golf in the summer. I had plans in showing her how not to play golf.

Family life was one of Mariah's main focuses. She was a holiday girl who looked forward to decorating her room and house for each upcoming holiday. Much to the chagrin of her parents, her preparation was sometimes months in advance. She enjoyed dinnertimes and was a helping hand to her mother in the preparation of weekly meals. She especially liked to tell comical stories of previous dinners and holidays. A zealous planner of family vacations, she took on the role of advisor to make sure we embarked on "Mariah-approved" destinations. During her transition from adolescence to teenager, she somehow still enjoyed being around her parents, even spending time with us in public. She traveled with us to many of my work functions and attended several conventions. Those sacred times of connection and communication remain extra special to us.

Janice and I were so proud of our little girl. She was coming into her own and was truly becoming a joyous young lady. Our hopes for Mariah were for her ebullient personality to expand, and for her to live a life of accomplishment and self-respect. I was so proud when our little girl weathered turbulence and used it to ground herself. She was the thoughtful counselor, the negotiator, and the energetic weekend planner for her circle of friends. Her band of merry girls and boys crossed the social boundaries between public school (Butte High) and private (Butte Central). Looking back at the qualities she possessed, I could see her going into the medical or counseling field. Due to her unique compassion for the injured and others on the downside of advantage, she might have become a nurse. Of course, as an avid Digger fan, her school of choice would have been Montana Tech.

On this October morning, this was our tight-knit family unit, two proud parents and two daughters who meant the world to us. Two daughters with a magical bond. Mariah was a close confidante to her sister, and Jenna welcomed the relationship. Inseparable as little girls, they had grown to complement each other as lovely young ladies. ❧

Our beautiful angel Mariah Daye

Family vacation, Oregon Coast

Family Christmas photo

Jenna and Mariah, sisters and best friends

Mariah, preschool graduation

Mariah's dance recital, age six

Leo's family birthday party

Mariah in kindergarten

Mariah in first grade

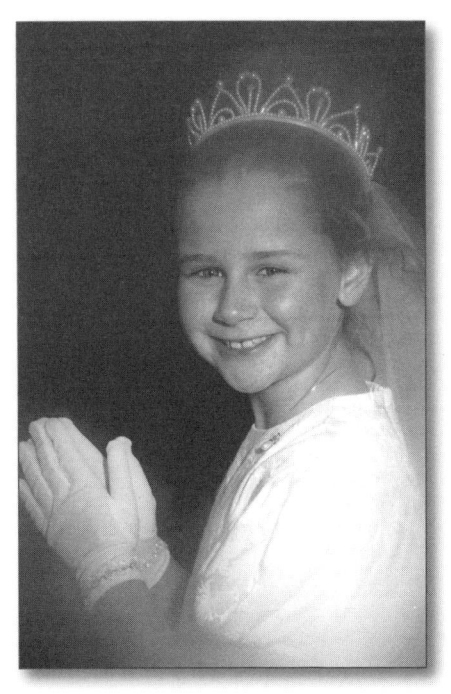

Mariah's First Communion

Mariah in third grade

Mariah and bowling team, the Strike Sisters

Mariah and Hillcrest School girls fourth grade basketball team picture

Above: NorthWestern award-winning Energy Share picture, 4th grade

Left: Butte's Christmas Stroll winning button, by Mariah McCarthy

Janice, Mariah, and Leo at Butte's Christmas Stroll

McCarthy Family Christmas, 2006

Cousins Christmas photo, 2006

*Above: Mariah,
06/27/2007*

*Right: Janice and Mariah,
Flathead Lake, 2007,
last family vacation*

Calm as it is, the fallen aspen leaves have caught a slight breeze and ridden it from the nearby golf course to land on the drying grass of my front lawn. Their deep brown veins and withered texture are the only summer echo to be found throughout the Summit Valley.

Truly, such an autumn morning is one of the best times in Montana. Crisp mornings that will nip the tip of your nose if you're not careful, and hot, dry afternoons just long enough to squeeze the remaining moments of escaping summer are how we like it. If there was a good enough snow the previous winter, the forest fires will be kept at bay under the skies of my home, which are among the biggest in the world.

Butte is not the Garden of Eden—far from it. But it is a fine place to start and raise a family. Many families are multigenerational. Even those who leave for far-flung places often come back to live here. ❖

2

INNOCENCE

When I am down, I must continue to believe she is near me, near us, as close as a breath of fresh air. I sometimes hold my own hand and delicately rub my thumb next to my index and middle finger in a circular motion thinking her hand is still there. I know she is smiling and holding my hand.

This story reflects a father's perspective, but my life would not exist, to say the least, without Janice, my lovely wife and the mother of our two precious children. Allow me to let Janice introduce herself:

"I am the middle child of seven from hardworking parents called Ed and Patty (Janhunen) Rademacher. My education began at Greeley Grade School, after which I went to East Junior High before graduating from Butte High. I attended MSU, and upon completing my first year enrolled in the local beauty school and started my career in cosmetology. I enjoyed my thirty years of working with clients, and with Shelly, Jolene, and Heather. My husband says he was my first perm attempt, a losing battle to cover up his follicly-challenged hairstyle.

"The man I married came from the "Hill," and his pride in his Walkerville origins is matched by his love of Butte. We were blessed with two beautiful children, Jenna Marie and Mariah Daye. Our little clan has had enormous love. Vacations, school plays with dance recitals, and grade school graduations made our family even closer.

"Little did I know that our family's strength would be challenged and our lives forever changed due to a sick choice from a faulty character."

Janice and I had overlapping but different relationships with Jenna and Mariah. As a father, I was resolved to not waste the opportunity to be part of their young lives. Mariah must have been about six when Jenna and I started bringing her along in the car to go running around town. I always loved time spent with my copilot. Listening to Mariah jabber nonsense was the best radio. The innocence of children in that stage of life is inspiring; a pureness of genuine curiosity is revealed with each question. These early years are when a man knowingly or otherwise assumes the most important duty of fatherhood: helping a child learn about everything around her, so that when she's able, she can safely and successfully navigate the world herself. Among the infinite ways parents affect their children, and the myriad hopes we hold for them, is the empowerment of daughters with the skills and ability to be independent, successful women.

Each of us is born without a bank of knowledge about our world, knowledge that as adults we take for granted; it is filed away deep in the recesses of the mind and assumed. The many moving parts with their own names and functions interact and create the life we experience and enjoy. I envy those "blank slate" looks that arise from innocence, those sponge looks where you can almost physically see a child's brain working overtime to understand an object not previously encountered. She is searching for a place within her web of current understanding; at times those objects fit in neatly, while at others they forcibly rearrange the foundation of all the child has known up to that point.

When thinking of this trait seen so often in my girls, I often wish for a similar sense of amazement from adults, based on a single interaction, conversation, or event, but it is rare among grown-ups. Potential, progress, goodness of perception—they all stem from such experiences. The key requirement for these sponge-worthy yearnings for knowledge to occur is an openness to wonder.

Mariah and I often found ourselves driving down Harrison Avenue, the oversized concrete ribbon making up Butte's array of box stores, sign pollution, and mini-malls. Buckled into the seat next to me, with the radio on but turned low, Mariah invariably would be transfixed by the outside world, as if it were a television screen to another galaxy that she was soaking into her mind's eye. We'd be sitting at a stoplight or slowing for a turn when her head would spin in my direction. A miniscule finger pointed toward the window and one of the buildings on the other side.

"Daddy, what's that?"

"Baby, that's a gift store where we can shop for presents."

"Okay."

Seemingly content with the answer, she would let her finger drop back into her lap as her attention turned from me back to the window. I can only assume that she needed a word to pair with what she was seeing out the window in order to label the image of the building and neatly organize her memory under "g" for gift store. Next time we passed a gift store, she would point it out to me.

"Daddy," she'd say, her finger rising again as her eyes turned to me, "what's that?"

"That's a gas station where we go to fill up our car with gas so we can drive."

"Okay," she said, pursing her lips again, the filing system at work.

And it continued like this as we made our way around town. Question, answer, contented daughter. The "What's That" game became a mainstay between us, evolving sooner than I thought it would from her asking all the questions to my quizzing her on buildings we passed. With Jenna, I had quickly learned how perceptive and intelligent she was, and now Mariah was walking in those very same footsteps. We have Janice to thank for passing on those genes.

On one particularly gorgeous summer morning, my copilot and I loaded into the car and began another round of errands. Midsummer flower baskets, overflowing with pops of red, blue, and white, hung from light poles along the southern half of Harrison Avenue. A million petals crawled down the sides of the baskets; they looked like Fourth of July-themed beach balls. At three feet in diameter, their striking explosions of color dotted the drab glass and concrete backdrop. I noticed small pools of evaporating water on the concrete below each basket. It was warm already, the air calm. The town had woken up, but on this morning the day's energy seemed to move more toward the "island time" side of the continuum than the East Coast side. Perhaps warmer temperatures do that to people, or maybe we use the heat as an acceptable excuse to move at a more sustainable pace. Regardless, on this American Dream painting of a summer morning, Mariah and I were headed to the store.

Not long into the ride, we began. She pointed, I responded. A book store . . . Dairy Queen . . . a flower shop. A few moments of quiet examination followed each. We then drove under the interstate overpass, the stripes of shaded concrete interrupting the brilliant early sunshine. The local radio station was on, and my friend Ron, the bubbly voiced and witty owner/morning personality, was reading "The Wacky Side of the News," a favorite of mine that highlights national shake-your-head-at headlines of stupid crooks and crimes gone awry. Stories like robbers sprinting out of a bank heist only to knock themselves unconscious by choosing to exit through the immovable side of a glass door, or of a criminal butt-dialing 9-1-1 when in the act. Stories of karmic justice, a guilty pleasure of sorts. I turned my attention to the radio as Mariah contemplated the view from her seat.

She was quiet, almost too quiet, that what-are-the-kids-getting-into silence. Suddenly, and without notice, she turned her head to me. She had a type of calm inquisitiveness that told me she was searching for an answer she didn't have. This time, though, there was no pointing out the window.

"Daddy." Her cute little voice rose at the end of the word as if that part was her question.

"Who knows me?"

I was slightly taken aback by such an interesting question coming out of left field, even for young Mariah. *Who knows me?* is such a loaded question. I thought how to respond: her inner circle of family first, proceeding outward from there.

"Well, babe. I know you. Mom and Jenna know you."

She looked at me, almost hanging on the next word, as only Mariah could do in her typical matter-of-fact curiosity. I paused for a second, hoping for some feedback. Since she hadn't interrupted or redirected me yet, I thought I must be on the right track, so continued: "Grandma and Grandpa Rademacher. Aunt and Uncle Bennie and all your cousins. Cousin Jessica is one of your best friends. Remember playing with her?"

With each person I listed, I could see her little mind working, making connections, as she seemingly checked people off some kind of mental list. We talked about our family, those we share holidays with and are fortunate to see often, as well as more distant family members we see less frequently. They were more of a stretch for Mariah's mind, but when I offered context on where we had last seen them her furrowed-brow confusion melted away into a contented half smile. She was eager to hear about and think of these people not in the car with us. She loved family, and being with family, and I realized something in my search for more names. She wanted to always be with the ones who knew her, to be with them in place or time.

After listing the names of a few kids she had played with, my old memory started slowing down, and I sensed her attention was, too.

"You see, Mariah? A lot of people know you and love you. I bet we even missed a few."

She turned her head, giving me a tight-lipped smile, and shook her curly hair head back and forth a few times. The list would suffice. This was her satisfied, *good answer Dad, I believe you* look. Nothing more needed to be said.

Once again, Mariah's head turned toward the grit-speckled car window to take in the sights of her town, our world. ❧

*C*losets in Butte are a contradiction manifest: shorts next to down parkas, snow shovels leaning against lawn mowers. This is typical, even expected. Montana weather is notorious for changing on a whim, and the threat of seeing all four seasons in a day—sometimes in an afternoon—is regularly carried out. All seasons are tangible in October. You almost count on bringing your mittens to the golf course or having snow pants in the back seat to put over your board shorts when watching a football game.

On this October morning, Butte is still in shadow, or it was when I got lost in my thoughts and first cup of coffee. Now the sun has started to peek over the East Ridge, its rays cutting across the valley and illuminating the Pintler Mountains to the west. Above the majesty of the East Ridge, the sun continues to climb. Omnipresent, the East Ridge rises precipitously from the valley floor. The Ridge's dominance has a personality of its own, echoing and simultaneously creating the mood of the city it watches over: hard, stubborn, and subtle. Sprouts of pine, aspen, and sagebrush paint its dramatic wall, and resilient, stately, and unyielding light kaleidoscopes against the dark. Echoing the area's complexity and mystery as it comforts those inhabiting the harsh landscape, the East Ridge also provides the pedestal for the landmark ninety-foot statue "Our Lady of the Rockies."

All in all, a storybook backdrop to the city that is, undeniably, "the richest hill on earth." ❖

3

Game Day

I didn't go into her room that morning to wake her up. I regret it now, but I am glad I did on so many mornings in the past.

From mid-August until late November, football is a form of oxygen in Butte. It's a very simple game at its root. As an individual, you do very simple things. You run. You tackle. You throw. If you execute each of those actions, you might be successful. Combined and put into the context of an eleven-man team, with the intricate complexities of positioning, angles, matchups, strategy, and timing, these skills belie the "dumb jock" stereotype, making it seem like a feeble attempt at belittling a realm of which one is ignorant.

Thinking back now, I better understand that what athletes take away from football is not just about the game itself—the x's and o's. The value of football is embodied in everything one takes away from the field of play, from the endless conditioning, the practices when you have no energy to continue, the mind-numbing position meetings, the off-season weights, and the guidance offered by the coaches. You may not recognize this until your cleats are gathering dust in a basement box, and you may not ever realize it. But if you are lucky enough to understand and grasp the essence of football, you will see it as a carrier of values.

When the athletes at Montana Tech pull their green home uniforms over their pads and look into the eyes of their teammates, I am reminded of the core and lasting reasons sports exist. All members of our family are staunch Tech boosters, for layered reasons perhaps exceeding my limited ability to describe. Each game I attend at Alumni Coliseum, I search for one of those special moments. I'm blessed that they do in fact reveal themselves to me.

Typically, it is a split-second distant recollection of how the game has shaped me into the man I grew up to be. I am reminded of being part of a team and of a rich tradition. It was on a field in high school that I learned how valuable I can be as an individual within a group, how my God-given talents can contribute to something bigger, and how I possess a certain and useful skill to further a common goal. I learned what I can achieve with persistence and practice, and that I can be emboldened by hardship, strengthened by those around me.

When I was in the trenches of the game, I wanted to be the best football player I could. My goals were that narrow. But now, I realize I did not play high school football simply to excel at a game, I wanted to learn the values necessary to turn the raw metal of my youth into the measure of a man, father, and citizen. I had the opportunity to play for coaches and with teammates who continue to be role models and friends, and I have benefited in ways I am sure I will never totally grasp. Walking off those fields, stained with grass and blood on jersey colors I shared with my brothers, was an absolute honor. No special talent on my part, just hard work, and I was glad to be part of a team filled with much better players and also to play against better players.

Those thoughts ran through my head on October 27, 2007, as I saw the Orediggers emerge from the locker room, like a swarm of resolute bees, across the manicured grass and pine trees to the gates of the field's hallowed ground. In the stands, green-clad youngsters ran up and down the aisles in search of friends, and the coeds sported small temporary M-T tattoos on their cheeks as they scurried around in their celebratory collegiate haze. The cheerleaders jumped and bounced; their energy was molasses thick. It was good to be a Digger, with the sun burning brightly over the emerald field sitting a mile above the sea.

The Orediggers came out swinging against the Bulldogs. Our squad wasted no time in doing what it has for eons, methodically grinding down a tough opponent. No razzle-dazzle, just Butte tough blue collar work ethic. Any team hoping to best Coach Bob Green and his old-school Orediggers has to earn every morsel of victory, play by play.

As the second quarter clock ticked down to zeros on the scoreboard beyond the south end zone, fans showed their support and adversity through throw cheers and comments. About the middle of the quarter, I headed down to the barbeque to assume my unofficially official position at the grill, flipping hamburgers and hotdogs. As always, the tailgate area was manned by the Touchdown Club, made up of former Orediggers and other Tech stalwarts. At my post, I was soon engulfed in grill smoke and chatting with Digger faithful stopping by to grab a bite.

Our area quickly ballooned into a mass of humanity, per the traditional half-time migration from the stands. At the same time, a line of people I did not know walked out to midfield in Tech apparel. The announcer read their names and every so often one of them waved to the crowd. It was hard to decipher between the crackling PA system and the noise coming from the group surrounding me.

Tailgates are a great time to laugh with friends you see often, and catch up with ones you don't, those who may only come to town for the games. Conversations often start with a handshake and small talk—the kind of banter that gets you up to speed on family, work, and home life—and nearly always circle back to the game. Despite the seeming insignificance of such exchanges, a tailgate gathering forms a bond that keeps the faithful putting on our faded green clothes each Saturday, donating to the school, and bearing the frozen fall morning preparation before the crowd arrives. Tailgates are opportunities to connect.

Then I experienced a moment that has been emblazoned in my mind ever since. As the fans' conversation about how to win the game came to a lull, I saw Mariah weaving through the crowd. She only came up to the middle of my chest, so she would disappear behind someone in the crowd, then reappear in an opening as she navigated through. Earlier, she had called to see if I had any money on me—a fairly typical conversation with a teenage daughter. I like to think I assumed the role of "ATM machine" with grace, and even took a bit of pride in it. Grabbing a handful of extra bucks for the kids in the morning is built into my daily routine. We had agreed to meet at the field before halftime.

She bopped through the crowd, her hair bouncing with each step, her eyes glowing in the bright midday sun. Somehow, her innocent beauty struck me just a little bit more than it usually did.

The people, the music, the cheerleaders, the wisps of grill smoke all faded into the background. It was just her and me—father and daughter. As I handed over a few dollars for a hotdog and a drink, I asked if she was having fun. Then I gave her a hug, kissed her forehead (one of our routines), and told her I was so proud that she was my daughter and Jenna's sister. Looking back, there must have been a time when the stubble on my cheek scratched her. I don't know why I thought of that, but I did.

She blushed a little and lingered in my fatherly embrace before walking off. After the kiss, I remember smelling her bouquet of hairspray and perfume. It was lovely. As I watched her disappear into the crowd, I marveled at how grown up she was getting, and at the elegance she so effortlessly exhibited.

To someone watching us, it would have seemed a brief, typical interaction. But what one cannot see from the outside was my rising emotion. In that moment, I was bursting with pride, with love for my daughter, a bounty I could never have imagined. As I wiped a tear, I was overwhelmed, and thanked God for both my daughters.

As Mariah walked away, she retraced the same steps I had taken when watching the Orediggers as a child. They were also the same steps her grandfather had walked when he coached here for all those years, pacing the sidelines not far from where we were that day. I had so often felt my dad's presence. As a child I would watch him instilling values in his players, leading by example. There. Here. Then. Now. In that realization, I felt the link between generations, and felt humbled that God had bestowed on me two of the greatest honors a man could ask for: Jenna and Mariah. ❖

*L*ife changed around here forever in the mid-1800s, when just to the west of town a settler found some curiously shiny flakes in what would soon be called Silver Bow Creek, after its sparkling resemblance to the ribbon of an actual bow. The eager prospector traced the creek through sage and timber groves, back to its headwaters on the Continental Divide. Those small flakes turned out to be the first fruits from one of the richest loads of heavy metals ever found in America.

Copper built Butte, which flourished. But now, over a hundred years after its rise to power, the physical city is a hollowed-out shell of its former glory. The remaining headframes stand prideful and resilient, yet abandoned, relics littered with ghostly memories. They join a skyline of half empty storefronts and mostly vacant towers reaching skyward.

But that is only part of the picture. Significantly, we also have institutions of higher learning, which have given us sport teams worth rooting for. Local pride is never in short supply, but it definitely becomes supercharged during football season. We love to win, sure. Who doesn't? Still, even our losses, both on and off the field, can bring us closer together.

4

The Voicemail

She was in a good place with her self-image. She was no less or better than any other girl her age. She was cute, attracted to boys her age, and a magnet of fun with other girls. She wore her heart on her sleeve. I drove off whispering I LOVE YOU—and I still do.

The game ended in a 28–21 Oredigger victory over the Bulldogs. Smiles all around.

We did not linger. Grabbing what was left of my tailgating ensemble, I headed through the crowd to meet Mariah and her friends at the car, where I repacked it like an oversized game of Jenga made of coolers, hotdog buns, and people.

Exhausted and happy, with the smell of grilled brats and overcooked burgers still emanating from our pores, Mariah, her friends Valarie and Kaitlyn, and I once again folded ourselves into my little PT Cruiser, Val and Kaitlyn bundled up in back, Mariah in front next to me. We headed east so I could drop them off at Silver Bow Pizza, the current teenage hangout spot and a Butte institution known as much for its games and indoor carousel as for the cuisine. The outside resembles a Big Top; red-and-white vertical stripes and large bulbous details outline the roof. Inside is a cacophony of circus music, pizza grease, and infectious laughter. On many occasions I had watched these same three girls converse and giggle or set up a possible spit-wad World War III from adjacent booths and tables.

I always found it a little funny that teenagers chose this particular destination. It didn't seem to me to fit the part; it was more a Chuck E. Cheese-like cliché than a teenage rendezvous. I suppose dad wasn't "cool enough" to understand. Regardless, we made this trip often, and the restaurant served as a reminder of the innocence and joy of youth.

When we pulled off of Harrison Avenue and into the parking lot, I could feel their youthful excitement. They were getting greedy to start their night, to be capped off with a slumber party at our house. They spilled out of the back seat with hilarity. Val and Kaitlyn were in the throes of an animated teen conversation, getting tangled up and spilling out onto the afternoon-warm asphalt. Mariah flashed me a quick smile and a thank you and leaned over to let me hug her and give her a kiss on her forehead, which was as special to me as kissing the Blarney stone or embracing the palm of a queen. To her it was likely the best way of appeasing her father without messing up her makeup. I rustled up some extra dollars for her, and watched her catch up to her friends, bopping over the concrete and across the parking lot. Seeing those three together, innocent and carefree, I was content. I gained a sense that all was right and just in the world, and the universe was eagerly at their beck and call. Author and pastor Max Lucado says that humans are pleased with eternal events that are seared into our hearts and souls. This was one such event.

I enjoyed seeing Mariah in her element, looking back at her two friends being klutzy and unleashing a belly laugh. She had that usual gleam of unspoiled delight. I could only guess she knew the day was turning into a night of possibilities, and that after the fun all three would end up at our house.

There is a time when teenagers have difficulty and turmoil just trying to fit in. I always hoped this phase never touched Mariah. If it did, it was not something she held onto. She was maturing into a radiant young lady, assembling her own world and acclimating to life as a freshman; and in her hazel eyes I saw her mother's beauty and a smile echoing that of her sister. My youngest was the culmination of all I treasured in the world. A father's time with his daughters is too often fragmented into a million pieces, so moments like these are ones that linger.

I remember telling Mariah for the billionth time that I loved her and to call for a ride when ready to continue her other planned exploits. Until her body passed by on a gurney to be loaded upon a Life Flight helicopter, it did not hit home that my brief kiss, my look into her eyes, and her smile of contentment were the last I would ever have.

Back home, I unloaded the car in the garage, a task I have never minded. It is integral to the tailgating experience, which allows me to hang out with friends over food in a parking lot. As always, I took pride in making sure all items, once cleaned, were placed back in their particular places, either in the garage or basement. That way, preparing for the next home game is easier. I have always enjoyed the rituals associated with football—the pregame ones, midgame in my cleats as a high school coach, coaching on the sideline in khakis, or supporting the boys from the tailgate and stands—and yes, even the postgame chores. Sometimes my tailgating gear would get mixed up, or I had trouble finding items the girls had put in places dad did not, but mostly my tailgate activities went like clockwork.

As the last cooler found its home, my mind turned to the coming evening. I was going to a gathering to celebrate the win over the Bulldogs. After touching base with Janice to make sure she didn't need me for anything, I chatted with Jenna and her sophomore crowd, then phoned Mariah and her two friends, drilling them

The Voicemail

with the usual parental protocol she'd heard a thousand times: call me or Mom if events change or rides are needed.

At the get-together there was an air of confident bravado. Senior football players were reveling in the joy of accomplishment, mingling and joking with former Tech players, boosters, and coaches. Some of their girlfriends listened to stories of sporting boldness and shook their heads, mostly in shades of disapproval; others gathered in the corner, telling their own versions. A few proud fathers stood with their chests out and hidden tears, reminded of their own rites of passage, as mothers breathed sighs of relief that their boys had made it through another contest with only nicks and bruises, escaping a major injury, by no means unheard of from football's violent combat. This blend of diverse roles and camaraderie went on into the night, pleasantly.

I called Janice, who was unwinding at home, to ask if she would like to come out and enjoy the night with some good people. I told her how my cheeks were tired from laughing, and suggested she would enjoy the silly charades from the even sillier characters. Already in her comfy clothes, she opted to stay home. We reviewed our daughters' evening itinerary. Both Mariah and Jenna were with their friends at a house of people we knew. I hung up and put my phone in my jacket pocket.

The night relaxed into the time when some made plans to continue their revelry elsewhere, maybe even start another round of festivities, while others began the subtle preparations to head back home. The partygoers were older, and responsible, and arrangements were made for designated drivers.

What seemed like only moments later, a lull came over the conversation, and I could feel my phone buzzing. I actually heard the vibration before feeling the buzz; my coat pocket and shirt must have been a barrier to sound. I looked at the screen: several missed calls. I was dismayed. When you have two teenagers, you are always on duty. Sneaking over to a quiet corner, I attempted to listen to the first of four messages. It was Jenna. Her quiet voice said simply, "Dad, Mariah's been in an accident, come to the hospital." ❖

*B*utte and its riches were built on the rippling stalwart wills and strong backs of the miners who worked the long, dangerous shafts thousands of feet underground. As the city rose out from the mines, the identities of its inhabitants rose as well.

Soon after the discovery of copper, the rush was on to capitalize on it, and as the century came to a close the tent-city of Butte erupted into a cacophony of frontier boomtown encampments fueled by tens of thousands of miners, streams of money, rampant lawlessness, and prostitution, all drenched in seemingly endless veins of precious metal. In the blink of an eye, the city's Uptown core took on a look more Midtown Manhattan than wild, untamed Montana countryside. By 1910 the thriving cosmopolitan city, named after an unmistakable landmark hill ejecting itself from the fields to the west, became the biggest economic powerhouse west of Chicago.

On a human level, whether it was a rickety steel cage lowered a mile beneath the surface, the shedding of blood and sweat in the tunnels connecting shafts, or payday—or a funeral—a palpable sense of brotherhood reigned among the mining-town shacks and headframes dotting the landscape.

Today we live in a far different world, with modern conveniences and institutions, including hospitals where our children are born, and where we are cared for when serious illness, injury, or tragedy strikes. ❖

5

BEDSIDE

Words do not sooth or medicate. Some, though, make a pillow against the oncoming dump truck of emotion.

I remember staring at my phone, the words reverberating.

Mariah . . . accident . . . hospital.

The background blurred, the noises melded into nothing. In the midst of a joyous crowd, I was alone.

Mariah . . . accident . . . hospital.

I don't think my disbelief was as long as it is in my memory; maybe a minute at the most before I gathered myself, forcibly keeping the worst possible thoughts at bay. My logical brain took over, telling me it was most likely a fender-bender and she probably had whiplash, the kind of manageable soft tissue injury in which the victim is taken to the hospital as a precautionary measure. It couldn't be more than that, this was my Mariah, and we had done everything right that night as parents.

Every bit of my attention was across town at the hospital. I closed my phone by rote and had difficulty putting it back in my pocket. My hands were shaking. I felt lost, foreign, as if my soul were preparing me to see the unbearable, while my brain resisted the urge to formulate those kinds of thoughts. I was stuck in the middle of two immeasurable forces. My body did not know how to react.

In my years in the insurance field, I had seen thousands of these situations, where almost always worst fears prove unfounded.

All I absolutely know at this point is that Mariah is at the hospital. It is probably something small. Nothing terrible could happen to our Mariah. Everyone else must be on their way to the hospital too.

My hands were trembling, my mind racing. I couldn't focus on anything but those three words.

Mariah . . . accident . . . hospital.

I looked at my trembling hands. There was no way they could control a car in this state, so I asked my friend Kevin for a ride to the hospital. He agreed without hesitation. Looking back, this was one of the first examples of community graciously offering us support.

Another friend, Chris, came along with us. The hospital was on the upper west end of town and we were on the lower south—a ten-minute ride up the hill. As we drove north on Montana Street, I was thinking and praying at the same time. Actually, I couldn't differentiate between the two, logic and faith. I did not know if my mental script was directed at God or meant to calm myself down. Maybe it was meant for Him, and maybe not, but it helped me gather myself and calm my mental storm.

I tried to imagine the longing looks of pain from Mariah as she lay on a hospital bed with an IV in her arm. I was thinking of the words to say that would comfort her while the medical staff went about their business. I was also trying to formulate words to say to Janice and Jenna to assure them we would get through . . . no matter what. Not knowing anything was the worst. I was directionless and tried to believe that all the possible scenarios were far-fetched.

The orange glow of the aged street lights blurred together, as did the homes and streets we passed climbing the road to the hospital. I shifted in my seat as we turned left onto Porphyry Street and toward the entrance to the hospital. In the midst of a million thoughts, I noticed how bright the moon hung on this clear, cold, dark October night.

We pulled into the St. James Hospital parking lot. The red EMERGENCY sign near the entrance grabbed my attention as soon as I could see its hue from the road, each letter screaming at me. I hurried, almost a full run, through the cold air biting my skin. The automatic doors made an eerie scratching of metal on metal before we could see the crowded waiting room on the other side. There was more activity than I expected, with many people pacing, praying, and waiting. An anxious, scared, anticipatory buzz spread throughout the room, as if we were all preparing ourselves to hear news we couldn't yet believe. Everything was making my blood boil, my heart pound, my anxiety rocket.

I scanned the waiting room. So many familiar faces, but I had laser vision to find only two—my Janice and my Jenna. Janice I saw first; she was wrapped in a yellow winter coat sitting in a row of chairs along the outside wall. We locked eyes; she had been crying. Before I took a step, I was hoping for some kind of nonverbal acknowledgement of Mariah's condition, a message from a mother's intuition. Janice wore a muted partial smile, not out of happiness, but of calmness because I was there with her. As I wrapped my arms around her, she said she did not know anything about Mariah's condition. Jenna sat by herself, mute, fighting back tears.

After coming home at midnight, her Saturday curfew, Jenna was the first in our family to learn the scope of this horrible event, when Valarie's mom, Peggy, called and asked if Valarie was at our house. After Janice relayed the news that the three girls were walking their friends home, Jenna went out to the porch, where she saw an orchestra of flashing lights. Walking down to the crime scene, she found it full of police and paramedics. Inching closer, Jenna saw a foot and recognized the toe polish she had applied for Mariah earlier that day.

Though I knew many people in the waiting room—family, friends, Mariah's friends, and members of Valarie and Kaitlyn's families—we did not talk much initially. The assembled either gave way to a concerned father, not knowing what to say, or were enveloped in their own grief. (Later, when I was escorted to see Mariah, I saw Valarie and Kaitlyn in their hospital beds, with their parents at their sides. Exactly when I learned that all three girls had been hit by the same truck I don't recall. I remember being informed by an officer who came to the ER.)

Determined to get some answers, I weaved my way through the crowd, toward the receptionist window, to find out our Mariah was fine. She had to be. I asked about our daughter's condition and if I could go back to see her, the whole while thinking of words to say to Mariah. *My poor fourteen-year-old must be scared out of her mind.* I wanted so much to be with her, to hold her hand, and to tell her *it will be alright.*

"Mr. McCarthy, the medical staff is trying to stabilize her, and I'll let you know as soon as you can come in."

Mariah . . . accident . . . hospital.

Time was irrelevant. I went back to sit next to Janice and told her what the receptionist said. I couldn't shake the word stabilize. It didn't sit well. That was a word used to describe dire situations, not simple whiplash. The words unspoken gave me a sense of confirmation of the serious circumstances. It sent my mind whirling as I fought within to force more positive thoughts: *She'll be fine, maybe more internal injuries that first anticipated, maybe a few more months of rehab. She'll still be fine.*

It was all a blur, a nightmare replay of scenes from Hollywood hospital dramas: the lack of information, uncomfortable seat cushions, the stark fluorescent lighting. Thoughts also intruded from my experiences with death insurance claims. The edges of my vision narrowed to a tunnel. My world now entered in that building and nowhere else. The lights. The floor. The receptionist's window. Chairs. Mariah.

My emotions begged for permission to be released, so I could cry my heart out, but my head kept telling me that I needed to be strong for my family. Vulnerability and strength faced each other down. I sided with toughness, thinking *that's what Janice and Jenna need from me right now.* I also wanted to help the others in the waiting room, who were frightened and worried beyond imagination. When you are sailing through a storm and your captain seems undaunted, you see that example and gain your own confidence needed to continue. As a father, I felt like I should play the captain and show strength, faked or otherwise. It was what we all needed.

A young nurse walked down the short length of corridor to the thick wooden door that divided the ER from the waiting room. Through the small vertical window in the door we could catch a small sliver of moving figures. It didn't amount to much, shadows really, but we would have grasped onto anything at that point. I knew I was not alone in my monitoring of any comings or goings in that direction.

Not long after I had spoken with the receptionist, a nurse entered the waiting room, and we turned our wet red eyes to her as she scanned the crowd. Seeing Janice and me, she started in our direction. We both perked up at the prospect of possible answers. Her every step caused my heart to quicken, my blood pressure to rise. So many images rushed before my eyes of what we might see on the other side of that door. Our baby, our beautiful, vibrant fourteen-year-old was all alone in there.

"Mr. and Mrs. McCarthy, I can take you back to see Mariah now."

We agreed that I would go in first and come back to get Janice and Jenna. I squeezed Janice's hand, hoping our connection would give me the strength we could muster between us. As strong as I thought I was, my insides were rubble. My stomach was knotted. Nothing of my fake sense of strength remained; in fact, it was Janice and Jenna who gave me the strength to rise from my chair. I looked at them both briefly, watery eyes meeting watery eyes. Hoping to wordlessly reassure and comfort them that I would return with good news, at the same time I had a sense—we all did—that the news would not be so. As I turned to meet the nurse, my mind darted between words and images so quickly it did not feel like I was even walking, but instead was floating only feet behind the nurse taking me to see Mariah.

Quicker than I imagined, we reached the heart of the emergency room, where a hive of health care professionals were darting from curtained room to curtained room. It was a larger room, longer than I had expected, with a middle command center dividing one wall of beds from the opposite wall of beds and idle machines. This headquarters was full of computer monitors displaying medical measurements and graphs, and equipment and supplies. Workers were stirring about with concern written on the creases of their eyes. They must have been engaged in organized activity, but I could not tell one way or the other. People moved hurriedly and purposefully in all directions with a variety of devices or handfuls of gauze.

Along the opposite wall were a series of rooms divided by pale cloth separators hanging on tracks from the ceiling. Each room was occupied, but I could not tell by whom. Maybe on slower nights these dividers were slid back against the wall, but not tonight. Based on our path of travel, I assumed Mariah was behind one of the divided partitions on this closer side. There was a different energy here, on the other side of the heavy, waiting room door, though I couldn't quite figure out what kind.

I kept thinking that the scene unfolding was something from a television show, something you hear about, or see dramatically portrayed as you flip through the channels on an uneventful evening from the comfort of your couch. Not something that would ever happen to me. I was having an out-of-body experience.

I remember the first sound of cries and whimpers I recognized as such, though I could not locate their source. I followed the nurse to a curtained opening. The seriousness crashed down on me when she stopped there.

My baby is behind this curtain.

My stomach dropped. I hesitated before entering. I could hear a mild mechanical hissing from the other side of the curtain. I instantly knew it was the unmistakable sound of an oxygen machine. My stomach dropped and I could only muster short, abbreviated breaths. I pulled back the curtain and met a fear beyond my worst comprehension.

Machines. So many machines they almost formed a wall between me and the bed. There seemed to be tubes everywhere, all heading in the direction of Mariah. Her swollen face, beautiful and silent, lay on the hospital bed pillow, unconscious and nearly unrecognizable. She seemed dwarfed by the machinery—things I had never seen before. My eyes traveled along the plastic hose taped to her mouth, connected by a metal pole behind her bed to the hissing, wheezing oxygen machine. Among all the others, this machine solidified the gravity of the situation. The machine would hiss going up; Mariah's chest would fall. An immediate wheeze would go down; her diaphragm would rise with life-giving oxygen.

My legs refused to move.

My little girl could not breathe on her own.

My baby girl was helpless.

This realization slugged me in the gut. None of my imaginary scenarios had prepared me for this. Mariah lay on the hospital bed, distant, gone, lifeless, only here by the graces of medical technology. Each tube attached to her, each hiss from the machine, drove a dagger further into my heart, twisting and tearing my soul to pieces.

I was helpless too.

It boiled in the pit of my stomach, my heart rising into my throat. There was no air in me. I gasped, wanting more than anything to change places with her, to take her pain away. I wanted to hug life back into her. On top of the sheet, her right hand was so pale it was almost transparent. She seemed so frail, so young, so innocent. I squeezed her fingers hoping some of my heat, my own pulsing blood, would pass through into her. Then I surrendered completely, my eyes erupting at the bedside of my dying daughter. ❖

*W*hen the shift whistle blared, hardworking men felt solidarity in the sinews of their limbs. This camaraderie, whose legacy endures, spilled out of the mineshafts and into close-knit neighborhoods. The vibrance of their stories is never far from conversation.

Each neighborhood had its own traditions brought over from a far homeland, creating a rainbow of cultural diversity unrivaled in this part of the world. Each played a role in forming Butte, where grueling work and the constant closeness to possible death let miners know who they could depend on when life in a hard-rock mining camp became almost too much to bear—one another.

From a parent's perspective, however, I came to realize, to my cost, that our town is also the bearer of another, persistent legacy, of cyclical alcohol abuse and a tradition of acceptance of drinking as an inevitable rite of passage for our youth.

6

WE GOT HIM

Our cries rose, determined, and then quietly drifted away like tides in a sea of grieving.

I stood frozen, sucker punched and dazed, with one hand on the edge of Mariah's hospital bed so I could stay upright. The texture and coldness of the sterile sheets gave me shivers. I was hunched over and heaving, gasping for air. My tears fell onto the plastic tiles making up the ER floor. No matter how hard I blinked, this picture did not change. It would be with me forever.

"She is only fourteen... She is only fourteen," were the only words that came to me. Breathless and weak, my body could not catch up to my fear, and my mind engaged in a feeble game of catch-up it would never win.

When I slowed down, the monotonous rhythms of Mariah's breathing machine overtook the sounds of my own gasping, my own search for air. The slow pattern of sound strangely calmed me, and I found myself timing my breathing with hers. *Hiss . . . pause . . . hiss.* The pattern was enough of a constant to allow me to gather myself for the moment. My sweet, giggly Mariah looked as if she were asleep.

No one had explicitly told me how dire her condition was, but somehow I knew. When the ER doctor said we needed to have her looked at by a neurosurgeon, I remember calling relatives and asking for a priest.

Mariah is still here. She's a fighter. She's a McCarthy, dammit.

My thoughts turned to Jenna and Janice, I needed to be strong for them. I knew I couldn't protect them from this reality, but a new thought crept into my mind: *Mariah isn't gone.* This slender reed of hope gave me what I needed to face my family. I clung to that thought, repeating it over and over. I whispered it to myself so I could hear the words on my lips. I screamed it in my mind with the love of a thousand fathers. If I said it loud enough, if I said it enough times, it would become true.

There we were, just Mariah and me. She was hurt, sure, and badly, but I would be with her until she could go home with us. No one and nothing could prevent me from being with my little girl. My errand buddy and Janice and Jenna and me, we would leave this hospital as a family.

Hiss . . .

Whir . . .

The breathing machine snapped me back to the present. Each hiss scoured my soul, reminding me that Mariah could not breathe under her own power. She was not gone, but I could not deny what that meant. I needed to face Janice and Jenna. To open up a gaping nightmare in which we might never find relief. But how? Words seemed futile, and added to the crushing weight. My mind was spinning out of control.

What do I say? How? I knew the words were a Pandora's box, and as soon as I opened it, the cursed contents within would set us on a course of horror and grief. My two rocks, their worlds would change forever. Simmering somewhere below the outrage and hurt, regardless of the outcome of Mariah's health, I already knew the box had opened, that our lives had already been irreversibly changed.

God, help me. I'm not strong enough to carry this news. I need the strength of a thousand mothers and fathers. I need the strength of Janice and Jenna. Something, God. God, please help me.

I leaned closer to Mariah. Just below her left eye was a window to her ever-radiant cheek, contrasting sharply with the many colorless tubes. I touched Mariah's cool cheek to let her know I would never leave her. I must leave now, but only for a moment. I would never truly leave her. Ever. I hope she knows that.

I turned to the curtain beyond the foot of Mariah's bed. Beyond that thin veil of dangling cloth was a waiting room where my beloved family—Janice, Jenna, and Mariah's grandparents Ed and Patty Rademacher—sat.

Dear God, give me the strength.

I navigated through the ER as well as I could remember, hugging the wall on my left side, reaching out for it to steady my crooked path. It was a blur. My vision had collapsed into a darkened tunnel fixed on the floor. In the background, the mechanical beeps, hushed conversations, and inaudible groans faded into white noise. One foot forward, then another. Each a step closer to the waiting room, to my family. This cross I held was breaking my will.

The storm of thoughts and the tornado of emotions must have been written across my face. When I reached the wooden door to the waiting room, I locked eyes with Jimm Kilmer and Shane Ford, who were both entering the ER corridor as I was walking the opposite direction.

Jimm's daughter Valarie had been hit by the same truck that hit Mariah, as had their friend Kaitlyn Okrusch. Jimm and Shane's faces were pursed, brows furrowed in looks of concern. Concern but resilience and strength.

I wanted to—tried to—say hello, wanted to ask about Valarie's condition, but my mouth could not form the words. I was a ghost, empty and distant. My lips moved, but my words echoed my ghostly self. My breath was stolen; I couldn't manage a sound. My eyes hit the floor.

Shane broke the silence. "Leo, we got him."

My tunnel vision snapped back to the present, to those two men and those four words. *Got him? What does it mean? Who is he? Why did you get him? What are you talking about?*

My eyes went from the two men back to the floor, from the floor to the wall, in an attempt to grasp the message. I must have been mouthing these questions silently to the world; they were spinning around my mind even more furiously than ever. Nothing seemed to fit together. Jimm could see me trying to come to grips with what Shane had said.

I imagine that in the moment I had the same blank look I cherished so much about young Mariah when she was trying to comprehend new pieces of information. As fathers, no doubt Shane and Jimm recognized this moment of disconnection, when my own web of understanding tangled as I searched for a way to make sense of the world.

Jimm broke the silence. "It was a drunk driver who hit the three girls. We got him."

His stone-faced demeanor lined everything up. I had been so focused on Mariah, on her condition, that I had not even considered the cause behind all this horror and uncertainty. My priority, my every thought, had been Mariah and her alone. Until now. I remember leaning into Jimm and Shane at this time; they were holding me up for fear of my collapsing.

My thoughts had never veered toward who had hit Mariah and Valarie and Kaitlyn. Kind of odd, but it had not entered my mind.

Drunk.

Driver.

Stunned, my mind raged with images of the three girls, giggling on the sidewalk on their way home. They'd had an eleven p.m. curfew, and after reaching our house had asked Janice if they could walk several friends home, a few blocks away. At the time, not knowing the details of the vehicular attack on these three innocents, I pictured three girls simply walking home on a pedestrian path. Under street lights. Crisp air. Mariah's last thought as a truck careened into all three. Twisted metal piercing human flesh. Trash on the passenger seat. The sound of the three skulls on impact. Police lights.

Kaitlyn, Valarie, and my Mariah hit so hard they were knocked out of their shoes and left for dead in the blood-stained grass on the side of the road.

Six empty shoes.

It was dizzying. My knees buckled and I stumbled into Jimm, feet unsteady, my mind a cacophony of white hot rage. My anger at this senseless act by I knew not who engulfed everything.

I looked up to see Jimm's face. He was holding me, one hand on my shoulder, the other on my chest. I felt the pressure, the connection. It somehow felt like the first human contact with the world without. Both our worlds had become a rubble pile of pain, and yet he offered a hand to help. These hands were real, tangible. This was larger than me, it was larger than all of us, and I knew I was not strong enough, no matter what I told myself. At that moment in our shared moment of desperation, his simple act of empathy and understanding may have saved my life, may have given me a sense that enduring this nightmare was possible.

Pain dripped from the corners of Jimm's eyes. I could see he was hurting just as much as I was. His daughter Valarie was in the room next to Mariah.

That moment with Shane and Jimm seemed to make the physical act of breathing easier, and their worried faces, their genuine hurt, the shared grief made the weight more bearable. My eyes moved from Jimm to Shane and back again as Jimm steadied my weight back onto my feet. I felt a tinge of strength sneak back into the recess of my being. It felt foreign, like it didn't belong in this world. But I knew that whatever would come of this night would be something none of us would go through alone.

I emerged from the harsh white of the hallway to the equally callous fluorescent-lit anxiety of the waiting area. The heavy oaken door opened slowly. There were too many people; it was difficult to cut through the crowd to find Janice and Jenna. Some sat in pairs, one consoling person rubbing the hunched shoulders of another. Some sat alone, with thousand-mile stares of disbelief. Every set of eyes was glossed over by fear or dread, probably both. Even in the midst of so many friends and family members, I felt like I was swimming in the middle of an ocean: emptiness beyond the horizons.

I am not a self-conscious person, but I remember noticing that my eyes were scratchy as I reentered the waiting room. The feeling you get after crying. I saw Janice, beside our good friend Shelly. She motioned for Jenna, still sitting a little ways off, distant and quiet in her own disbelief, to come over. When I met Janice's eyes, my vulnerability rose up in my gut like a beach ball choking my airway, again preventing me from being able to talk. And when I tried to look into Jenna's eyes, it was too much for me.

My eyes welled up, and heavy tears spilled onto my cheeks and shirt. I released the shackles of masculine pride and let my vulnerability explode. I gasped. We cried. We hugged each other. The gravity of what I saw did not need to be spoken. They knew. We all knew. We were an island of wordless consolation, prayers, and grief.

When I could gather enough breath to utter words. I told Janice and Jenna that we could go back to the room, but that they must be prepared to see the unimaginable. I tried to explain that Mariah was medically situated, unable to talk. My voice cracked at the effort it took to shape each word. I simply had no power to describe what was happening any other way. There is no book, poem, or essay to draw on that can express that your daughter lies listless on a hospital bed.

Due to an underage drunk driver. A murderer behind the wheel.

We stood up, my princess, my queen, and me, and started our procession down the longest, loneliest hallway to ever exist.

We turned right into the ER and the row of partitioned rooms. I could hear sobs behind curtains from Valarie, Kaitlyn, and their families. Their whimpers will always haunt my nightmares. Between these searing painful sounds, we could make out abbreviated words to the medical staff on hand.

We silently walked into Mariah's room, where a nurse was replacing an IV of antibiotics that was soon swinging from the small metal pole. My heart yearned as I pulled back the curtain to reveal Mariah behind all the machinery. Jenna moved to Mariah's left, her eyes fixed on her sister's face. Janice moved to Mariah's right. I was at the end of the bed. Mariah's toes were exposed through holes in her torn socks. They were scrapped and crusted with dried blood, but you could still make out her bright nail polish—the polish Jenna had helped her apply earlier that day.

The mechanical hissing was still methodically breathing on Mariah's behalf. *Hiss* . . . her chest would rise. *Hiss* . . . it would fall. I noticed one hazel eye was slightly open; her beautiful left eye peered out from behind those majestic lashes. (Her eyes, blue as a child, later turned hazel, which prompted an ongoing family discussion!) We stood in silent understanding, processing what was before us. Tears would erupt quickly and disappear just as fast. Janice, always the devoted mother, broke the impasse, leaning in and taking Mariah's right hand. A compassionate touch, slow, deliberate, loving. Janice was gazing longingly into Mariah's eyes as if to say *we are here*. Then she leaned over, taking Mariah's left hand and joining her two hands together, gently placing them in a cradle on Mariah's stomach. Janice, Mariah's hero, and everyone's Rock of Gibraltar.

We were powerless. None of us spoke, surrendering to the situation. Tears fell. Our cries rose, determined, then quietly drifted, like tides in a sea of grieving.

It wasn't long before my familial senses clicked. We are a close family, but that also includes our extended family. With the gravity of the situation now palpable, I motioned to Janice that we needed to inform Patty and Ed, the girls' grandparents. When Patty answered the phone, I was unsure of the words that would escape me. I cut right to the point, avoiding unnecessary pleasantries. I told them that it did not look good for Mariah, and that we needed them to help pass along the horrible news to other family members. After I hung up, another wave of severity passed over me. Once you begin to let your family members know, to spread the news outside of the room, it becomes more real. More final.

When I returned to Mariah's room, a doctor was explaining to Janice and Jenna that there was no neurologist in town, and that based on Mariah's weak brain wave patterns the doctor of record was unable to make "the call." I felt like my soul was being slowly ripped through my heart with fish hooks of disbelief. The pace at which everything was happening was dizzying. In a matter of minutes, seconds really, my family's life has been forever changed. My mind traveled back to Blacktail Lane, picturing the crunching of glass, the reflective road barriers dividing the traffic lane from the sidewalk, the solid thud of three girls colliding with all that metal, each strand of lovely hair flying wildly through the air in slow motion.

The next day I would learn from Shane Ford, who came to our house to deliver the news, that the guilty party was underage and drunk and behind the wheel of a sizable truck. The girls had never seen headlights swerving as the truck approached them from behind. And I learned the driver's name, which I did not recognize.

One block from home. MARIAH and her TWO FRIENDS were hit by a DRUNK DRIVER ONE BLOCK AWAY FROM HOME.

But in the moment, at the hospital, I was focused only on Mariah. She was still with us, barely. That morsel of hope was enough to cling to. *She's a McCarthy, and she's gonna fight like hell.* ❧

*C*lusters of ramshackle homes sprang up near their respective mines, and an oasis of a capitalist, industrial city, whose success set it drastically apart from anything within a thousand miles of western wilds, was forged from its singular neighborhoods, which had their own parishes and watering holes.

Family life thrived as the Irish Dublin Gulch, Centerville, Corktown, and Walkerville grew together with Finntown, Italian Meaderville, Slavic East Butte, Butcher Town, the McQueen Addition, and Chinatown, which was next to the burgeoning Red Light District, the southern border of Uptown. As neighborhoods filled in, eventually there was nothing separating these areas but waste-rock piles and culture, and Butte became an American melting pot.

Religion helped establish a social and meaningful contrast to the 24-hour bars, wide-open casino gambling, and openly accepted sensual pleasures for a price. It was not uncommon for a miner to leave a drinking establishment to attend Mass. ❖

7

LAST RITES

*M**y faith serves as an inner light, bracing me in the face of daily tribulations and concerns. Faith and the hope of any spiritual table droppings of grace remain things to hold onto. We held onto each other around Mariah's hospital bed, heads bowed, stifling cries, in prayer, trembling with tears dripping on the bedsheet.*

Already in overload, we listened to Dr. Frank Raisler, a kind man whose reassuring eyes were rimmed with tears. With patience and firmness, he carved through the heavy fog of death stinking and slinking into the far corners of the room, an unsaid storm cloud looming along the western horizon. We all saw its presence but did not want to acknowledge it.

The care by a team of professionals, young and old, came to a plateau; they had done all they could to stabilize Mariah, and decided to contact the Life Flight helicopter from Missoula's St. Patrick's Hospital. Once the Life Flight had been decided, Jenna and Janice left to update Grandma and Grandpa and ask them to continue to circulate the grim news to our extended family.

When I looked at the sweet eyes of my Mariah, sadness rose to an almost unbearable level. I tried to will the tape and tubes to disappear from her skin, and to believe that the rising and lowering of her chest was a result of our playing basketball together in the driveway, not the forced intake and exhale by machine. To transform her hair, matted red with gravel and blood, to merely being covered with sweat and dirt from helping Mom garden in the backyard. With every fiber of my being, I wanted the cacophony of hospital sounds and weeping to melt into the breeze among the aspen leaves on a warm summer afternoon. She lay there, innocent. A child. I believe I did my best for her as a father. I hope she believes the same.

I grew up in a Catholic household. My faith has been a guide, an atlas of action and wonder, dating back to family prayers in front of the Virgin Mary statue that sat on a special place on the piano. And having been an altar boy and gone to Catholic school, I am no stranger to the pageantry and calisthenics a typical Roman Catholic Mass entails. Religion classes drilled the Seven Sacraments into us, and one that was spoken of but never experienced, Extreme Unction, which is now called the Anointing of the Sick. It is to bring peace to the dying. Mariah was unable to have the complete Last Rites. That holy event is called Viaticum.

One October Night

The three sacraments are Confession, the Anointing of the Sick for a conscious ill person, and Final Communion.

The time had come, and I asked for a priest and was briefed on what would happen. As the priest gave Mariah the Rite of Extreme Unction, Janice, Jenna, Patty, Ed, and I approached the hospital bed, holding hands as the deacon prayed and delicately and respectfully anointed my sleeping angel with holy oil.

After that, the quiet reflection inside Mariah's curtained sanctuary quickly exploded into an orchestrated and methodical haze of motion. The plan was put into motion, and experts converged. She was in the hands of the specialists. I was asked to leave as they prepped Mariah for the flight, but politely declined, taking a step backward. I didn't want to leave my little girl but needed to give the medical workers their space.

I wanted so much to simply pick Mariah up, squeeze her like I had done hundreds of times, and carry her out of the nightmare and into her bedroom. Still it was necessary for me to step back, both physically to allow the nurses and doctors space to do their jobs, and spiritually. On reflection all these years later, that step may have been the one by which I released myself and let God take over. My helplessness became palpable and it became clear that whatever happened to Mariah would be in His hands.

Within moments, Mariah was cut out of her clothes and her motionless body was secured in a cocoon of body wraps and blankets. The nurse handed me the pile of clothes. I mutely accepted the tattered gifts. I was not ready for this simple moment. These were clothes that Mariah chose to wear before she was mowed down and left for dead. I looked down at what had become of Mariah's night, and felt the texture of her jeans and the cotton of her jacket, noticing the contrast of bright colors. The bundle was heavy with blood and bits of flesh I thought to be my beautiful baby girl's brain matter.

Memories flooded back of my singing an off-key misquoted Irish lullaby while holding her, in her pink swaddling clothes, the first time, softly welcoming her into the family, the clan, and the world. Memories of sitting quietly next to her bed during one of the many days she slept in, my right arm around her left shoulder as I spoke softly in my role as a fortunate father: Make it your day, be yourself and get dressed, you have fifteen minutes to get dressed, eat, and go to school!

I wasn't handed any shoes. They were still at the crime scene. As I came to learn, they were found nearly fifty feet away from where Mariah and Valarie and Kaitlyn lay. The thought of the three of them struck so hard that they were ejected from their own shoes sickened me.

I felt the stomach punch of grief and the throat punch of uncertainty.

As the ER staff prepped our girl for the flight, my good friend Josh Vincent met me at the exit door and embraced me, asking how he could help. I remember walking up to the waiting helicopter with Janice, Jenna, and Coach Green. At the sound of the chopper I felt a brief moment of sympathy for him and my other Viet Nam vet friends, hoping it did not bring back bad memories. I felt like a paper airplane in the calm center midst of a hurricane,

When the helicopter door slowly shut, the look of assurance from the Life Flight crew buoyed my tortured spirits, if just a little. As my little angel was heading over the city she loved, the gust of the slowly rising copter kicked dead leaves and brown grass into a whirlwind around our small group behind the safety fence, and my mind wandered to winter days sledding with Jenna and Mariah on the front lawn of St. James Hospital. The ritual of dressing, the cajoling of bundling up, their combined symphony of laughter as the sled started its descent, ending with cheers of excitement as the sled flipped after hitting a small bump. Pulling the two girls back up the hill seemed strenuous back then, but I would gladly do it again many times over. ❖

Around 1920 the population of Butte peaked, then started to decrease as new techniques and technology replaced the need for underground labor. The mining headframes and towering steel structures built to lower miners into the bowels of the earth made way for a gaping open-pit mine and haul trucks, so as to remove the rich ore as quickly as possible. By the 1970s our town's prestige and economy had lessened further; more affordable copper came from overseas, which paralleled a shifting national economic and cultural climate. Nearly all the mines closed, abandoning nearly half of the town. Layoffs decimated the workforce and by the early 1980s all local mining operations had shut down.

To add to the boomtown's bust, a focus on environmental awareness settled into the country's consciousness. During Butte's all-consuming drive for copper at all costs, the Anaconda Copper Mining Company had been seemingly unconcerned with mining's effects on the surroundings. When the Environmental Protection Agency established the Superfund Program to clean up hazardous waste, Butte and environs became the largest Superfund site by area in the country.

Mariah and Jenna were to be part of the latest generation to witness and participate in the inevitable changes, for better or worse, in our part of the world. ◈

8

MISSOULA

The city where Mariah placed third in her age category for the whole state of Montana—it was her first year bowling!—a good city, became the place of departure for her, and a place of solemnity for us.

Phone calls to our extended family, quick showers and frantically packed overnight bags became a blur. Janice's brother Dan took the wheel as we headed down a moonlit I-90 in our Chevy Suburban, which had taken us on countless trips and vacations. Now it was a taxi of dim hope and fear. Thoughts of could've, should've, would've stabbed my mind as the moving silhouette of the moon reflected on the landscape, bringing pangs of grief for Jenna and Janice and their silent agony. As the lights of Missoula came into view, I asked myself, *How will I muster anything resembling a father's strength to support my loves?* Fleeting thoughts of our plans for a family vacation to Ireland disappeared as the night gave way to the early western sunrise.

St. Patrick's Hospital rose before us like a European cathedral. Arriving, we saw the Life Flight helicopter, silent as a hearse after delivering its human cargo. Electronic doors whizzed open, recalling a familiar memory of a Walt Disney ride. On *this* ride the terror was real. Void of people, the solemn lobby was staffed by a woman with a sympathetic smile who must have met countless families in similar situations. Death hovering, with different backstories. A nurse led us to a small side room painted soft brown, its walls hung with Montana nature motifs. My mind wandered to the majesty of our state. A somber-faced neurosurgeon bid us to sit. Around a small table were positioned the three McCarthys and the doctor and his worry-eyed nurse.

He did not waste time with pleasantries. "Mariah has no medical chance to survive and you should think of organ donation. She suffered such irreparable damage to her brain that life isn't sustainable. We have her stabilized and on life support. You can go visit her after we complete the process." Words do not adequately describe the heavy silence, the evacuation of oxygen, and the unstoppable realization that this nightmare was a waking one. I lost control of my senses and lacked the ability to wipe a cascading torrents of tears. *Our baby girl, Jenna's lifelong sister soul, is not going to ever rise from her bed and be with us.*

An elevator brought us to a brightly lit hall in Intensive Care, where nurses were doing everything their training prepared them for to assist us and our little Rookie. Mariah had many nicknames, some made up in the moment, a few private ones that slowly came to mind. She was a hesitant girl who always wanted to know what the situation was before jumping in. As a baby, she clung to her mother, preferring soft, loving care to the clumsy handling of her father and the whisker burns from his hugs. She admired her big sister, and would laugh roundly at Jenna's jokes, always a willing participant in her big sister's many planned and impromptu plays. This play, with its unwilling actors, had no curtain to reveal it as make believe. No Faustian or Shakespearean lessons, no heroic miracles.

We were formally introduced to the medical staff and immediately felt like we had known them for years. Kind hearts, expert care. Like St. James, St. Patrick's Hospital is a place of professionalism and concern. When we were directed to one of the many rooms that would house our forever-fourteen Mariah, a movie began to play in my head, a montage of episodes of walking into the girls' rooms. The home on Sunset Road where we started our little clan morphed into the temporary rental apartment on Hobson, and then to Holly Lane. Tiny faces with big smiles during bedtime rituals of reading. My silent midnight walks down the hall to lean at their doors, listening to sounds of contented slumber, and to give thanks for our lives together.

Mariah was lying on the bed. Machines whirred to allow her to breathe, and water-balloon-sized IV bags dripped life-sustaining liquids into her unmoving, fragile body.

Jenna moved to her right, grapping her delicate hand. Janice was murmuring Mariah's name, as I stood at the base of the bed trembling and rubbing her little like-elf toes. The stillness was deafening. Our lives had contracted to a grim point, this small room. My heart pounded and bounced against my ribcage. Our three souls were being ripped and torn through our hearts. An *I love you, Mariah* chant changed to *We love you, Mariah*. Our soggy, hurting hearts fused together at her final bed.

As I was walking listlessly to the restroom down the hall, a nurse stopped me, her eyes misty with tears, and asked if she could do anything more for us. I smiled, gave her a hug, and slowly replied, "All we wanted to do is to grow old with her."

We waited in Missoula as Mariah's body's valiant fight gradually ebbed and her response to the collision from the Ford truck and the subsequent landing on cold asphalt started to show. About this time, Bob and Karen Bennie, Janice's sister and brother-in-law, arrived from Spokane. Bob and Karen provided physical and emotional support when most needed, as did their daughters Jessica and Nicole, respectively Mariah's buddy and Jenna's sidekick. Their presence gave us a welcome reprieve from our raging rivers of pain. The word grateful seems inadequate to express our feelings of gratitude to those who came to St. Patrick's to be with us, some named here, some not. Relatives, friends, and peers. Their persistence in staying with us, hugging us, and not leaving until Mariah's body was prepped for surgery, was overwhelming.

As we grieved, life went on. Outside these walls the recreational activity that is autumn in Missoula would be in full swing. Walking, biking, and enjoying the last warm days are a recipe for end of October fun. No doubt a few hardy late kayakers on the river attacked the rock-strewn torrents.

Bedside, Mariah's picturesque face began to blemish due to her cranial injury, and discoloration diminished her divine countenance. Her half-shut eye gradually closed. Lost was her unique look in a face approaching demise.

We decided to donate her body to help others. Janice, Karen, and I were ushered into a small side room to complete the paperwork. Karen was needed as a witness. Signing our parental power over to Life Center was not painless or pleasing. We were giving her body to help other hurting souls, moms, dads, and children enduring a life of detours and delays due to medical complications.

Our youngest's organs were to be harvested, an odd term, at best. We were effectively signing over our rights to our forever fourteen year old. Movies and daytime soaps cover this event but only from the outside.

Once our signatures were dry, word went out to possible recipients. Mariah's death would give them a chance to live. And it did. Mariah's liver allowed a little girl to become a big girl. One of her kidneys went to a man who was able to go home with his family. Her other kidney went to a fourteen-year-old girl. Her hazel green eyes let others see the rising and setting of the sun. Her skin went to numerous burn victims. Her pancreas and lungs contributed to diabetes and cancer research.

Back at Mariah's side, we saw that her face had begun to swell from mounting cranial swelling. Gone were her leprechaun dimples and rosy cheeks. Her hands were slightly cold to touch and kiss. Between the replacement of IVs that were keeping her organs alive and our final goodbyes to visitors, we slowly began to pack, hastily, our overnight bags. Even as our sentry duty over Mariah slowly ebbed, Jenna stood vigil at her side, softly caressing her hand and calling her name, while Janice intimately gazed upon her younger daughter, gently stroking her hair.

I witnessed these enduring acts of love through clouded eyes, my soul silently pleading to take their pain away.

Death is a singular common dominator; it binds superstition and belief. As we neared the inevitable, the seconds, minutes, and hours blended into a tapestry of tears and hugs. Memories of a young Mariah drifted through my head: her infectious laugh, the inquisitive twinkle in her hazel-green eyes. We held hands and said goodbye, kissing our gal one last time. At the nurse's station, our caravan gave final thanks, then as the sun started to set, we left Missoula, returning to lives forever changed. ❖

*O*ur oversized boulevards hold a fraction of the automobiles of yore, and weathered signs hang from neglected buildings whose ornate architectural details cling to time, waiting for the stroke of a paint-soaked brush and the trowel of a skilled mason. Every corner has a story, each brick holds a memory, and the broad streets and sidewalks whisper tales of the lost past, shadowy memories that live on in photographs.

Roller-coastered theme parks, crisscrossing trolleys, and boisterous feather-boa'd theatergoers—this all was once Butte. Old-timers speak of bustling streets, businesses full of patrons, and the ease of affluence. Ask them about the glory days and the stories you'll hear, replete with revered bounty, will typically fade or trail off, leaving in their place the crumbling brick and mortar of the present.

Cheek by jowl with our enduring camaraderie and undaunted strength of spirit is something else, however: the inheritance of vices associated with Butte's mining camp adolescence, the widespread, firmly entrenched tolerance of erratic and excessive debauchery. On that score, let me say unequivocally that it is time for a change. ❖

9

ROCKY WAVES

Mariah's room was a journey into her life. It was full of mementoes of her early years: her dolls, her plastic Disney figurines. Photos on the wall show her friends at many events, among them the Earth Shuttle Trip, chaperoned by the East Junior High teaching pair of June and Lloyd Magnusson and Rich Bertoglio, who traveled to Florida on a plane with forty eighth graders—and took them to the Kennedy Space Center and Disney World. The chaperones were living saints! Mariah's room was filled with memories. It will have no new artifacts of life after October 27, 2007.

How we got back I don't quite know, beyond that Dan Rademacher drove and that we made quick calls to family spread across the country. Driving down Blacktail Lane I was still trying to fathom how the "accident" happened. The more I found out, the more it would seem like murder. Was he trying to scare the three girls and lost control of his truck? Did he pass out? (All these years later, many questions still remain.)

Certain events make the reflection of society's mirror hard to accept. From my years in the field as an insurance adjuster, I had long been very aware of the evils of drunk driving and underage drinking. Now, the decision of what turned out to be a twenty-year-old boy to abuse alcohol and get behind the wheel had lifted any remaining scales from my eyes. For me, Butte lost its innocence when he killed Mariah and shattered the lives of Valarie and Kaitlyn.

Waking up in my own bed the next day beside the rhythmic breathing of my sleeping Janice, I hoped it had all been a nightmare. Sitting on the edge of the bed as the quietness of the house slowly evaporated, I struggled to stand. Mentally, the involuntary steps were hard, physically even more so. The vestiges of sleep were replaced by weary thoughts: *How do I go on? What steps can I take to rebuild a semblance of normalcy? How can my soul stop suffering and surrender to the bleak unknown?*

My grief was in its infancy. History is full of sorrow and pain and death, and we now know that the body changes from a constant diet of pain. You inhale, remember the pain, exhale, and become numb to your inner self-stoic, deaf to the intuitive voice that says to keep stumbling, fumbling, mumbling on. The sun still comes up, but its rays are less nourishing. Nonetheless, love remains the constant positive vibe the body fuels itself on, even as grief eats at your insides on a cellular level and invades the sinews of the flesh.

Before I had the courage to look inside Mariah's room, I positioned myself in the doorframe. Countless times, as fathers do, I had leaned against the entryway of her and Jenna's domains, where I would listen for the sleeping sounds of their merry imaginings. Often I would wake Mariah with fatherly advice to rise and shine. On special days I would sit on the side of her bed, with her head on my shoulder, holding her tight, offering my habitual encouragements.

Her room was exactly as she had left it the previous Saturday, her bed haphazardly strewn with clothes that had not made the cut for the day with her friends. Pictures of friends festooned the walls, her desk now eerily emitting the look of a museum. An overwhelming urge took hold and I brought one of her shirts to my nose. I wanted to imagine Mariah still with me—her fragrance, her giggle, her voice squeaking as I held her tight and eased up.

Plummeting to my knees at the foot of her bed, I muffled my scream and wail of WHY? Standing back up, I made my way to Jenna's room. The mind wants to progress from apprehensive disquiet to thoughts of those who are alive. I must have needed reassurance that life was still on my side. Outside Jenna's closed door, I listened for her sounds of sleep. Confirmation changed to a flood of memories of Disney video marathons with her. Under Jenna's guidance and tenderness Mariah's initial hesitancy toward new experiences had given way to burgeoning self-assurance. Abundant images of Jenna helping Mariah with coloring, math, and the production of plays made up on the spot came flooding back as well.

Starting the day meant checking my phone for messages. Friends from the past and more recent ones left consoling words, soft cries of love and support. Grief is never easy or comfortable to articulate. We were touched to find out that the day after the girls were hit by the truck, their friends had created a shrine near the area where they had been left to die. Butcher paper posted on the wall was covered with signatures, moving messages, and outpourings of love. Candles cast silhouettes of teddy bears and angel figurines—shades of an old black & white movie.

Over time, conversely, there were also some highly unpleasant developments. Certain people we did not know, and some we did, were shockingly heartless even this close to our tragedy, questioning our role as parents, and repeatedly asking why the three girls were out "at that hour." This hate mail from individuals who had no idea what had actually happened was often unsigned. Our daughter's ashes were still cooling as these evil clowns concocted their vile cards and letters.

Such behavior gave us an unwelcome peek into infantile souls. Later, a deluge of pathetic characters would assume the guise of Internet trolls in a chat room on the *Montana Standard* site. Some of the remarks were so toxic that periodically the paper had to close the site down.

I soon realized the need to protect my family from such filth, which came both through the mail and social media. "What was she doing out?" "You caused her death!" "Do you think it's karma?" "The kid is a really nice kid, he just made a mistake." "She will be in a better place now." "Why destroy another person's life by incarceration?"—that was another one, as if drinking and driving is a victimless crime. I suppose "re-victimizing the victim" (a phrase I learned in counseling) makes certain people feel better or exceptional or more sophisticated.

For some reason, a quote from Joseph Campbell comes to mind in response: "All the gods, all the heavens, all the hells, are within you." There was and is no gray area. A drunk young man murdered Mariah and severely injured Kaitlyn and Valarie. Nonetheless, the kindnesses of many outweighed the callousness and rudeness of the few.

And I never felt hate for the driver until days after our return to Butte, when Shane Ford filled me in on details, eloquently painting his own sacred, Good Samaritan acts of that night, and how he came to learn the facts. The driver had been a cold, calculating coward, leaving the scene of the crime. Over time, he would offer a menagerie of shifting alibis in an attempt to conceal his culpability. My initial fury was borne of the instinct to protect my family from a drunken terrorist. DUIs are that to me. Even so, I never wanted to act out my anger; my black belt training and my being a father stopped me. I did, though, rage against the night. In my tsunami of pain, I asked and prayed for help, for guidance.

For several months, and especially on holidays after family meals, I took long walks on the pathway of his carnage and down to Mount Haggin Drive, stopping and leaning against the stop sign, looking at his house, wondering about the atmosphere in his household. As I engaged in my silent reflections, I had no desire to harass or harm. My trail at the beginning of these walks was straight and measured, but on the return consisted of meandering footsteps while my emotions seesawed between grief for what I had lost and gratitude for the family I still had—for my precious Janice and my precious Jenna, and our lives of necessary adaptations and continuance.

Our return from Missoula had been met with visits from cousins and other family, who graciously brought meals with them. Neighbors came and went, with tear-filled eyes and consolation, and even more delicious home-cooked meals. Strained words of support mixed with snuffled cries and empathic embraces became common. People occasionally confess to not knowing what to say in distressed times, but showing up in and of itself is appreciated as a collective recognition of pain, grief, and hope; admitting that you can't find the words is understandable. All in all, the visits, cards, calls, and texts provided a haven and served to prop us up when our aching souls made certainty fade away.

As the week went on, my brothers, sisters, nieces, and nephews converged on Butte. Travel plans were made from California, Washington, Alaska, and farther away, and from nearby Idaho and other parts of Montana. The term "clan," with its many meanings, is part of Butte's cultural inheritance. Even distant relations and friends from early childhood, high school, and college offered their steady support. My peers and partners at State Farm were rock solid, too. In the violent, booming, emotional voyage of grief, human contact buoys the heart and mind. You never entirely clean up the mess that grief makes, a misery that like spilled coffee grounds can never quite be erased.

Books that explore grief emphasize that no stage is categorized or completely concentrated, that the transition between stages has no bright lines. The expense is weighty and the currency unstable. You screech into the wind one minute, laugh and shed tears of gratitude the next. One hard-learned lesson that came from it all was the realization that grace kicks grief's ass every time. ❖

The open pit eventually resumed operations and continues to be mined, despite volatile market fluctuations. It offers the same well-paying jobs for back-breaking work that Butte was built on, though far fewer of them.

Today, the town remains a furnace of character. Humility forms its backbone. We are proud to be a part of the great state of Montana, whose citizens live by a code of integrity and honesty. Although we no longer roast ore in open pits, Butte continues to work hard. Living here, in this community, makes us resilient. Hardly survivors, we are believers. We can do anything we set our minds to.

The only question is what that will be. I like to hope it includes no more tolerance for drunk driving, and no more dead children at the hands of underage youth drinking behind the wheel. ❖

10

PUBLIC MOURNING

How do you articulate what a fourteen-year-old daughter meant to your family and life? Her smile? Her laugh? How much Jenna and Janice mattered to her? Her pride in her Irish heritage? How do you convey what her girlfriends meant to her? Her enthusiasm for bowling, volleyball, basketball, and dance, and as a silent watcher of her surroundings? Her eagerness to join in with honesty and gentleness if she felt safe, and to hang back with reserve at other times? There are multitudes of definitions of who she was and what she loved while upon this soil in Butte.

When Mariah's friends and classmates congregated behind our home on a warm, soft autumn day, bringing posters and printed expressions of their love and their struggle with her sudden absence, I had no vocabulary of consolation to offer their eyes filled with hurt and doubt. There were cluster hugs and tears. But we did have optimism, that we could make something positive out of a very big negative.

After mingling, consoling, and thanking the parents, I climbed the steps of the deck and spoke from the heart. "We all hurt. We all have questions. One thing we do have is the hope that somehow good can come out of bad. Stick with your loved ones. Talk, cry, breathe. Life gives us lessons. One big lesson is not to drink and drive. So the next Mariah is not mown down without mercy. Thank you. We love you."

Next came the wake. The Irish Wake has long been common in Butte, an act of reverence for the deceased as much as a closure for the family. Though no dissertation or discourse exists to guide us through the mental gulag of an experience so public and private at the same time, in *My Father's Wake: How the Irish Teach Us to Live, Love, and Die*, Kevin Toolis writes movingly, informed by personal connections to mortality, and conveys the sanctity of the ceremony and how it helps both family and community members. He also writes of the extended experience of "normalization" and how we can find a way through and beyond the stage of angst.

The casket having been selected and our family wake scheduled, Janice picked out a favorite shirt of Mariah's. During the service last words of love were whispered and spoken true to our traditions. Chuck Richards and Denny Dolan had done a kind, professional job of preparing Mariah for the viewing, demonstrating

One October Night

respect for her, and doing so with grace. As the lid closed on Mariah, plans were in place for the Mass, to be held the next day.

The Mass was in St. Ann's Catholic Church, a beautiful, majestic neighborhood house of worship where Janice and I were married and our girls were baptized and both had their First Communions and Confirmations. That morning started early. I awoke to walk through the house, with birds chirping outside, their sounds intermixed with the muffled barks of neighborhood dogs. The day was slowly warming; the sun climbed over the East Ridge and remnants of low-lying clouds slipped away. The mention of clouds takes me back to the time I first drove Mariah and Jenna to Hillcrest Elementary. As I turned east onto Mount Haggin Drive, Mariah said that the feathery and white billows wafting across the amazing cleft of rock made her think of what Heaven would be like. She would have had her hand on her chin, with a small, pleasant smile on her face as she looked out the window. I would hazard a guess that she knows what Heaven is like now.

The house bustled, and friends came by to help us transport special items to the church. This being Butte, some also brought food. Coach Bob Green provided a signed football from the 2007 Orediggers football team. Holding the ball opened floodgates of memories of times spent with Jenna and Mariah at Alumni Coliseum. A draped green harp flag from the seventeenth century Confederacy of Ireland served as a table covering.

At the church, we welcomed the long visitation line of mourners, then Father Haffey started the farewell Mass, historically a profession of belief that death does not break the bonds with loved ones. The principle is a celebration of life, death, and resurrection.

In the Catholic service ritual predominates, to help the grieving, but also to show faith in the process and ending of life. Our family wanted to send a message of hope not hate, sanguinity not savagery, to illustrate who Mariah was to us and how she would have wanted to be remembered. We must have gotten that message across, at least to some. Several days after the Mass, my friend J. J. Perino sent me a heartfelt letter. In it he said, "I left St. Ann's that day with a different feeling. I felt good about myself and life in general. I learned a lot about the strength of people, and when times get dark, people come together." That's all we could ask, to transmit some life-affirming rays from the cavern of our pain.

During the ceremony, classmates read tearful poems of love and goodbye, and Jenna set the tone of love, sisterhood, and heartache. Outpourings of love, grief, and kindness filled the church, with people in the pews and standing room around

Public Mourning

its concentric interior. We had chosen two of Mariah's favorite songs: "Spirit in the Sky" by Norman Greenbaum and "Come Sail Away" by Styx.

Minutes leading up to the final goodbye were tumultuous and emotional. I did not want the limelight on me but on words of hopefulness, trust, and expectations. When "Come Sail Away" ended, I slowly made my way to the podium, stopping to genuflect in front of the main altar, then paused to kiss my fingers and gently place them on Mariah's picture. It was as if I were walking in a void.

There was no script, manual, or playbook to tell me how to speak about Mariah, my young flower of a spirit whose days on earth had been brutally cut short. Should I channel fire and fury and let loose the shriek of my broken soul from the pulpit? Or offer a small petition of optimism? There is no healing in spite, and I was resolved not to unnecessarily reside in misery and torment.

Making eye contact with Valarie Kilmer and Kaitlyn Okrusch, the driver's other victims, who were sitting in wheelchairs and visibly showing their pain of injury and loss of their friend, brought me back to the moment at hand. Seeing so many kind, grieving faces soothed my anxiety.

The word "eulogy" has its roots in ancient Greek, and by the time of Late Middle Ages was established in our own language. Mine came directly from the yellow legal pad Janice, Jenna, and I had worked on as they helped me to choose words to convey our family's difficult path of trust in change, and to express how we had let hate go by the wayside. Tattered, wrinkled, and discolored from countless tears, those pages immediately take me back to November 1, 2007, a calm day weather-wise. It was All Saints Day.

"Mariah loved that song."

I devoted the first minute to thanking those who had offered support from that horrible night to the present. So many people had helped during the fog of death. They know who I was talking about. Then I held up a phone book of Butte to illustrate the breadth of our community.

"To the man responsible for today, I look forward to meeting you to tell you how Mariah lived. For only you know how she died and only you know she could have been saved."

I held up a photograph of Mariah.

"October 28, 2007, is just a date, just numbers. A Sunday. I want to talk about the 61,961 days she lived.

"Mariah started that day with a good sleep, a special breakfast of pancakes from her wonderful mother. She went to the Tech game, kissed and hugged her father for the last time, and watched Tech win. Thank God! She hung out with her friends all afternoon and finished up at the Silver Bow Pizza Parlor and had fun.

"Mariah was born on March 12, 1993. From the start, she did not like to be pushed or hurried. I think this stems from having to be induced to come into this world. She had to be coaxed out to join her lovely sister Jenna.

"Mariah was later diagnosed with having a defective heart valve. The defect was organic, but it did not stop her from wearing her heart on her sleeve or sharing it with others. She felt it was not the size of the heart but what you do with it.

"Her interests were many: drawing, reading, and being with friends topped the list. At the time she was killed, she was with friends.

"She was a bowler and a dancer, she played basketball and volleyball. She loved being a Civic Center Psycho and wearing her 'Dirty Water' T-shirt.

"Our Mariah was a good, old soul, who liked harmony not drama, laughter not fighting. She had a unique and special bond with her "Poppa," Janice's father Ed Rademacher.

"Her funny character and loving personality come from her mother. She sure did not get her lovely hair from me.

"She was her sister Jenna's biggest fan, from serving as Jenna's footstool to playing Baby Pop in their Barney shows. She also was a co-conspirator in many goofy antics around the house. What Jenna was doing, Mariah was doing. Jenna, you were so patient with her, helping her learn her alphabet and fractions. I love you. Mariah could not have asked for a better role model, better sister, and better friend.

"Mariah latter teamed up with her best buddy, Jessica Bennie; those two raided the refrigerator together on many a night.

"Mariah had more Tech Digger memorabilia that I did, and she thought Coach Bob Green was cool.

"Mariah loved everything about her Irish heritage and Ireland. And she loved Butte, its history, and its people. She loved to hear stories of Grandpa Dan McCarthy's boxing and athletic prowess. She also would pass out from laughing at stories of Dad's lack of it.

"Mariah also loved to write. Here is a poem of hers from Legendary Lodge, a great camp."

We highly recommend Legendary Lodge; while there, Mariah became friends with Clay, a good kid and the son of Heidi and Mike Van Diest. Mike coached the Carroll Fighting Saints, and Mariah and Clay were resolute fans of opposing teams. She loved teasing him about that.

Public Mourning

The poem I read she called "Mariah's Song":

> It's Our Job.
> You will pray with him,
> Through the dark and light
> Just so you know
> Everything will be all right.
> We weren't meant to fight,
> We were meant to love,
> He just wants us to share his
> Word from above.
>
> It's our time to
> Make a change.
> We've got to put a stop to all the rage.
> It's the light inside
> That guides us.
> We've got to help those
> To see it our way.
> It's our job to spread the word of God.
> We've got to open hearts,
> We've got to fill them with love,
> We've got to help you see
> That he loves us.

I also read a letter she sent us: "This week at Legendary Lodge, my goal is to try to understand my religion more so I can talk and become one with Christ. I also just want to get away from all the nasty and hard things going on. I want to just be myself and have as much fun as possible. I'm just going to be myself and not hold back on my true personality."

I will miss our family rituals, but most of all I will miss the goodness Mariah brought to our family and Butte. ❖

PART TWO

My family's story is one that some may not want to hear. It involved, of necessity, seeking what justice is available when you have lost your daughter, your sister, forever. In our system everyone is presumed innocent until proven guilty. That system is a large step forward from the biblical retort of an eye for an eye, but it is far from perfect.

The prosecution faced a well-funded defense team that left no stone unturned in seeking to get their client off the hook for his unconscionable actions. Having no other choice, the other two families and mine saw the process through. We were there every step of the way, hoping for whatever small measure of relief sending a strong message to the perpetrator and the community could provide. It would not bring my daughter back. But it might help save the lives of other potential victims.

My views on the need to change attitudes about underage drinking and driving while intoxicated were crystalized long ago by Benjamin Franklin: "Justice will not be served until those who are unaffected are as outraged as those who are." ❖

11

CRIME AND CONSEQUENCES

I often turn to the Roman Stoic Epictetus, whose words serve for me as an emotional defogger. In his Discourses, he says, "Where is Good? In our reasoned choices. Where is Evil? In our reasoned choices." Mariah's killer was a sentient being. He had access to reason, and he made choices. The system's role was to hold him accountable. I believe in accountability. But like most of you, I had little knowledge of how that accountability is sought in a court of law. The following account comes from my attendance at court hearings, my notes, and public records. Opinions expressed are mine alone.

On December 6, 2007, a little over two months after the night an underage drunk behind the wheel hospitalized Kaitlyn Okrusch and Valarie Kilmer and killed my daughter, he pled not guilty to all charges: serious offenses against Kaitlyn and Valarie and the Vehicular Homicide of Mariah Daye McCarthy while under the influence. I expected nothing less based on his cowardly behavior after plowing his truck into those three beautiful girls. He protested his innocence with a false alibi, claiming that he was elsewhere, out looking for a deer by Roosevelt Drive.

At his arraignment, he was every inch a despondent man. My lovely wife actually felt sorry for him. This act of amazing sympathy despite his having left three young girls as roadkill on the cold asphalt of the designated walking path.

The legal walk-about started quickly, proceeding from an attempt to suppress evidence, which was denied by the Montana Supreme Court, to the argument that the coward should get a lighter sentence and skip prison and go directly to the Treasure State Correctional Training Center, to then be transferred to a prerelease setting with no time behind bars. This attempt to coddle an unrepentant criminal was denied and the case moved forward.

After one of the many court hearings, Linda Piccolo, who had been sitting in the gallery, introduced herself. Linda is a remarkable woman. She taught high school English and Theatre for many years and is the author of a number of plays. In addition to a smile that can melt an iceberg, she has a regal bearing and an infectious personality that comes with a laugh that makes you feel you've known her all your life. She attended most of the proceedings, taking copious notes, later

One October Night

supplemented with detailed interviews, culminating in her stirring one-act play about Mariah's murder and the way the case made its way through the legal system. (Illuminating excerpts appear in the back section of this book.)

The brutal, callous events of October 27 and the investigation and charging of the driver responsible having been covered in the local and area press, the defense was granted a change of venue. The prosecution continued to prepare its case as the families steeled themselves for trial in historic Roundup, Montana, just over 250 miles north of Butte. Ultimately, however, on advice of counsel the coward changed his plea to guilty, on four counts: leaving the scene of a fatality; vehicular homicide; and two counts of negligent vehicular assault.

On January 21, 2009, at his sentencing, the families were allowed to address him directly. Jimm, Peggy and Chad, and Margi expressed their feelings eloquently, and Kaitlyn Okrusch delivered amazing insights into her life after October 27, 2007. I spoke last. My Victim Impact Statement (reproduced largely intact at the end of this book) was passionate and pulled no punches.

Then the guilty party was allowed to speak. He was well coached. He picked up the lectern, faced the news media section directly and stated, "I wish I could remember all of this shit." He had just called my daughter "shit!" There was no *mea culpa*, no accepting blame. According to him, he had blacked out and had no memory of his crime. No sympathy, and certainly not any empathy for his living victims, and for all the members of the families.

Well over a year after taking Mariah's life, the now-adult and still-unrepentant young man was sentenced to twenty years in prison with ten years suspended. He also received concurrent ten-year sentences for hit-and-run and for the life-changing injuries to Valarie and Kaitlyn.

One memory especially has stayed with me from the many proceedings before the plea was made and sentence rendered. During the evidentiary hearing, a video was shown from the dash cam of Officer Petersen at the scene of the crime. It showed the mayhem at the scene. I was less than seven feet away from my daughter's killer and noticed no physical or emotional response from him. Then, during a break in the hearing, Mariah's murderer side-glanced and noticed I was watching him as the officer's video played again, on a loop. Still no sense of sorrow for the victims in his eyes.

A second memory is baked in disgust. During another break, those in the courtroom filed out onto the majestic rotunda of the Butte-Silver Bow Courthouse, where from the handrails you can overlook the frescoes in the ceiling and marvel at the workmanship and craft. Jimm Kilmer, Chad Okrusch, and I were on the south side of the opened rotunda discussing the proceedings, and as we looked to the mingling group of the defendant's supporters, we noticed him and his friends congregating at the east side railing.

He and his friends were laughing! Laughing. Unfathomable. And at a hearing during which the arresting officers had been detailing the night of October 27, 2007, and the coward's gruesome act. When he noticed us, he immediately got red-cheeked and slumped his shoulders and looked down at the ground. Joking around with his buddies at a murder hearing. Unconscionable.

* * *

After the sentence was imposed, the guilty party became inmate 3001578, and was escorted to his new home at Montana State Prison. You would think that the legal proceedings would then stop and hopefully some remorse would settle in, along with a resolution to be a better person or at least the bare minimum of being human. That did not happen.

3001758 did not serve his sentence with any measure of acceptance of responsibility. Far from it. Over the next few years, his legal team tried a series of legal maneuvers to overturn or undo the court's sentence. In March of 2009, 3001578 tried to have the remainder of his sentence suspended. As *The Montana Standard* put it, "Judge Newman denied his request amid testimony he was a 'below average' inmate at a prerelease center in Great Falls."

And on August 5, 2010, I had to put my surviving daughter Jenna's birthday on hold. 3001578 had requested a hearing, at the Montana State Prison, where one of his attorneys argued for a reduction of the sentence based on the emotionality surrounding proceedings at trial. Along with Jimm Kilmer and Chad Okrusch, I was permitted to express utter dismay at this brazen move. My statement started with my introducing myself as the father of a murdered fourteen-year-old and shaking hands with the new members of 3001578's defense team. I referred to the cold, calculating coward by his prison number. He had not, and never has, earned my respect to be called by his legal name.

I spoke in front of the three judges, stating that the criminal had not changed since the night he failed to render aid at the scene of the carnage he created, and that he remained the same emotionally stunted bully who would still be a threat should he be back on the street. Due to time constraints, I was unable to read Jenna's statement.

One October Night

Assistant County Attorney Mike Clauge delivered an excellent rebuttal to the defense's argument, one that proved his expertise and hard work. The ruling came back: 3001578 did not get to change his address.

Inmate 3001578 did complete the boot camp; he was by no means the valedictorian. He was then moved to the Great Falls Pre-Release facility, where he failed again to show even a modicum of responsibility, much less contrition, for his heinous acts. Yet again, he could not muster even a fake show of empathy or sympathy. His failed sojourn from the Pre-Release facility led to his being transported to Shelby, Montana's, Crossroads Correctional Center, where his behavior was sufficient for him to be allowed a parole hearing on April 25, 2012.

Jimm, his wife Peggy, Janice, and I made the three-and-a-half hour road trip. We were permitted entry and went through security. As we were sitting in the waiting area, 3001578's team showed up with his parents and some family supporters. The look in their eyes said it all. Despite all of the insensitive remarks, and the denial of my daughter's existence, and the life-changing assault on Valarie and Kaitlyn, we were not staying quiet. We would be heard, and I would fight for his taking responsibility for the tombstone above our daughter's body.

At the hearing, 3001578 presented himself as a changed person who had matured from a young misunderstood boy and become a man who prayed and wished alcohol would be wiped off the face of the earth. Members of his family also spoke in favor of his metamorphosis.

Jimm spoke eloquently of 3001578's lack of empathy and his non-acceptance of his actions. Something else was always to blame, never his own demented poor-me mentality.

Then I spoke of Mariah. Who will always be fourteen, a faded picture, a void in her sister's soul. I spoke of the constant lack of joy in our lives from that cold autumn night forward, of the soul-suffocating holidays, of having only three dishes at mealtime. I presented to the board a picture of Mariah, a copy of her birth certificate, and the ugly document 3001578 wrote: my youngest daughter's death certificate. I asked 3001578 to face up to and understand the collective and individual pain he had caused (and continues to cause to this day). From his blank stare and slumped position in his chair, I don't think I got through to him.

The return trip was melancholy, with highs (stories of our loved ones) and lows (the glacial splash of reality). Later, I was told by phone that the board had agreed to his parole. I accepted their decision. The caller suggested that I speak to youth about drunk driving and the consequences. I replied that I had been doing just that since 2008.

The Department of Corrections transferred 3001578 to the Butte Pre-Release Center, part of Warm Springs Addiction Treatment, & Change (WATCh), a mere twenty miles west of Butte. WATCh is an alternative to the traditional "lock 'em up" sentencing of adult felony DUI offenders. When I met the program head, Mike Thatcher, at the Pekin Noodle Factory, I told him of my regurgitation at the parole hearing, but also said that if his program could turn 3001578 around, it would be performing a service to the community.

I highly respect the work Mike and his colleagues do for willing inmates. WATCh strives to balance the best interests of those on the inside and those on the outside, based on a modified therapeutic community model of treating addiction and social issues. The regimen includes an intense cognitive behavioral program, and a Knights Program to help inmates convicted of vehicular homicide under the influence break through the armor of their many layers of denial, so they can to begin to rehabilitate themselves. Having personally seen the changes the program can accomplish, I have also spoken at the facility.

3001578 completed the program and was placed on probation under the supervision of the Helena Adult Probation and Parole, where I got to face him at a short meeting. Rose Everett-Martin, certified mediator and ardent supporter of the Victim Impact Panel of the Montana Department of Corrections Victim Programs, arranged this ninety-minute, face-to-face encounter. I have abided by the nondisclosure agreement and will only say 3001578 answered questions regarding his actions, including leaving the party on the West Side and his twelve-mile trip to Blacktail Lane. His story was radically different from his original "shit" remark. I have experience working with and confronting his ilk, I and left with no sense of his having taken the Knights Program's goals to heart and begun to deal with the horrific severity of what he had done and its consequences. I would like to say I caught even a glimmer of evolution in his heart and soul, but that was not what I saw or heard.

This impression is corroborated by Linda Piccolo, with her customary eloquence: "Prior to completion of my play, I contacted Montana State Prison, filed the required paperwork, and was approved to correspond with [the prisoner]. I think I naively believed he might want to represent himself and, I suppose, express remorse. I did so and rather quickly received a handwritten, two-page letter. It was rambling, full of grammatical and spelling errors, largely incoherent. He questioned my reasons for writing such a piece and what good could possibly come from it. He made no declarations of guilt or innocence nor any expression of remorse. I found it neither sad nor edifying, simply disturbing. That response is the reason his character does not appear in the play; nor is he named unless by witness or court statements. I did not then, nor do now feel any pity for him."

My own thoughts and gut sense of his lack of remorse and responsibility are based on his silence, which bespeaks a stunted worldview, one that is 3001578-centic. From the limited information available to me, I believe that as of 2020 he lives and works in Helena.

"When the call came in that night, a feeling of complete and utter fear overtook my entire being. I put on some sweats and my mom's yellow coat and ran upstairs. I told my mom what Lindsay had told me and we got into our Suburban and drove down to where the truck with the cracked headlight had previously been. Three ambulances and four cop cars had taken its place. People had already surrounded the area with tears rolling down their faces. Right then I felt the tears welling up, but I knew I had to be strong for my mom, who was having a harder time than I was."

* * *

"Mariah was only fourteen. Things like this aren't supposed to happen to innocent girls. She was my baby sister. Life without her will be hard, even scary, but I know she is always with me. Now I know what people mean when they say you never know what you have until it's gone. In that one day my life was changed forever, and if it's not the scariest feeling in the world to see someone in your family die before their time I don't know what is. She's out there, in a better place now, and upon hearing bumps in the night, I'll know that it's probably her just letting me know she's there."

–from an English paper by Jenna McCarthy

The Birth of Mariah's Challenge

*D*eath is viewed as a closed door. Mariah's death was a door slammed without warning, without her knowing it. But a door opened afterward, and was torn off its hinges. That door opened to bring good out from a very ugly bad.

The months following Mariah's murder were filled with anxiety, love, and the first stages of acceptance. Our family had been shattered, but we had to try to move forward. Mariah's death left a sister who was now deprived of her company. They had been able to talk, share wishes, and laugh like they could with no others. Her death left a mother's eyes brimming with tears as she struggled to understand that Mariah was gone. Her death left a father who spent long days at work on insurance claims and now had to complete and close claims on behalf of his first-born. And it left in-laws, adult relatives, younger nieces, nephews, and cousins to try to find words of consolation to ease their sorrow and our own.

Even as the legal case against Mariah's killer began to take shape, I had the thought of starting a foundation in her memory, to offer local youth the opportunity to receive a Mariah Daye McCarthy Scholarship. Our motivation was to support the young people who have been robbed of their innocence due to alcohol-related, preventable accidents and the immense, horrible pain to the survivors.

The scholarship, in Mariah's memory, would be an achievement equal to an academic award, one based on integrity and honesty; hopefully, it would encourage wide-open conversations on personal responsibility and the consequences of underage drinking by giving incentives to those under twenty-one not to drink by rewarding them with college scholarships.

If we thought things would go smoothly, we were wrong. Despite immediate positive responses from concerned parents, grieving friends, and others who wished for change and for the streets to be safe for teenagers, we were in for a tough brawl. We met resistance for going up against the local culture of winking at underage drinking and driving. Scoffers thought we would lose interest or simply fail. Like many in Butte, I had been in fistfights, though I was not proud of any of them. This was a different kind of fight, but equally bruising.

Part of the resistance involved the ugly posts and hate mail mentioned earlier. Even before Mariah's cemetery plot had been purchased, we were assaulted with these ignorant comments. Such low actions only provided fuel for me to continue, and over time the anonymous and pusillanimous remarks, and others by one-time friends, were replaced by strong pats on the back as we confronted longstanding social norms and "philosophies" about underage drinking and drinking and driving in general. It would have been easier to scorn and sow havoc, but our movement's resolve only stiffened. We were out to create a legacy of love rather than a monument to misery. Our goal was to transform the lives of my daughters' circle and the other young people in Butte.

The Copper Kings, who plundered the land's resources through the smelting of the earth's ore, created the concept of BUTTE TOUGH. We are known far and wide for hard charging on the ball field and not backing down from a fight. So, with Mariah's Challenge we decided to appeal to this hard-rock mining ethos, not for our glorification but to try to end a local and cyclical rite of passage. And let me be the first to admit that I was no saint in my early years, and though I never had a DUI, I was part of a culture that considered one a badge of honor and thought asking for help or a ride was an act of weakness.

By no means did we give birth to Mariah's Challenge alone. Early on, Bob Bennie and Tom Cronnelley took the embers and ignited the torch into searchlights on social media that started the conversation. The angel of design was Bob's sister Tish; others pitched in, with Jimm Kilmer and Dan Haffey taking the lead. Such unwavering support in the face of slings and arrows buoyed our spirits, as did a soul-hugging article by Leslie McCartney that helped to disabuse the notion that I was some kind of reincarnated version of Carrie Nation. Her article proved instrumental in paving the rocky pathway toward giving birth to a movement of change.

Michelle Shea's unwavering support served as a spiritual crutch, and Cindy Stergar and her husband Brian "Moose" Holland provided crucial assistance to establish the Mariah Daye McCarthy Scholarship Foundation, a 501(c)(3) tax deductible organization. Cindy also put together the first awards banquet to present scholarship winners.

Less than four months after Mariah's death, I presented the movement at the Butte Civic Center during a basketball game between the boys and girls of Butte High and Anaconda. At half-time I tried to describe the problem—yes, Butte, we do have a problem—that the Challenge addresses, then introduced our first board of directors, who received a standing ovation.

Dan Haffey of the Butte-Silver Bow Health Department also spoke movingly. His tireless belief in our cause was only matched by his ability to set up multiple area high school presentations. And Gina Evans's dogged support relieved much of the stress in the presentations.

The rest of that emotional night centered on handing out B.A.D (Butte Against Drinking) shirts designed by Kassandra Stenson Cossette. There were also "I Accept Mariah's Challenge" wristbands, angel pins, and window decals that served as artifacts of the "Grow Old" credo, and were accompanied by brochures and pamphlets. Kaitlyn's father, Chad, sang his own composition, "Angel Mariah." Valarie's father, Jimm, spoke stirringly.

Our early aim was straightforward, and it still is: to create an atmosphere where the twin scourges of underage drinking and drunk driving can be discussed openly in order to change Butte's cultural self-image as a place where anything goes.

Our movement spread its wings as Mariah's Challenge entered countless high school gymnasiums and hearts. We made a hundred-plus presentations across Montana and America, from Seeley Lake to San Bernardino, California, from Spokane to Chappaqua, New York. Nashville was a highlight, where we took part in the national conference of the Office of Juvenile Justice and Delinquency Prevention. The stories of the young people and their thank yous were what kept us going.

Lyrics from "Kyrie," a popular song written by Richard Page, Steve George, and John Lang, express our mission:

> *Kyrie Eleison down the road that I must travel*
> *Kyrie Eleison through the darkness of the night*
> *Kyrie Eleison where I'm going, will you follow?*
> *Kyrie Eleison on a highway in the light* ❖

13

Hitting the Road

Montana is vast. The term Big Sky carries a feeling of expanse and open ranges. Well-traveled highways crisscross this magnificent state of hardworking independent citizens. There are also frontage roads with weather-created corduroy sections, and roads made by the curious who go off the beaten path. The roads the Mariah's Challenge entourage has taken are less traveled and with no Siri to help. The journey has taken me all over the country. But wherever I go, I am always glad to come home again.

Our early presentations led to frank discussions. Tear-inducing accounts of family dissension and heartache propelled Jimm, Dan, Gina, Jon, Chad, and me onward. A spiritual bonus was seeing young people motivated to believe in themselves.

Some early recognition for our work came from the *Dr. Phil* show in mid-2009 when an episode called "DUI Outrage" included a short voice-over segment about Mariah and the Challenge. That same year, we were part of *People* magazine's MLB All-Stars Among Us, along with thirty souls who wake up each day and make the world a better place. At the game, I was awestruck on meeting Darrell Scott, whose sage advice cleared many dark clouds regarding the fears of starting a movement for our youth. After his daughter Rachel was killed at Columbine High School in April of 1999 (she was the first victim), Darrell had launched Rachel's Challenge to spread the message of goodwill and compassion. By sharing Rachel's story and inviting students to start a chain reaction of kindness, Darrell has changed lives and prevented suicides. An old saying, "When the student is ready the teacher will appear," describes my feelings about him. I will forever hold dear the moment we walked across home plate at the St. Louis Cardinals ballpark and high-fived in salute and pointed to the sky with beaming smiles for our angels above. I walk in Darrell's footprints on this adventure. A follow-up in *People* also shone a bright light on Butte, its courageous youth, caring parents, and gracious community.

At the MLB All-Stars Among Us, it was my good fortune to meet Richard Nares (who would become a Top Ten CNN Hero in 2013). This amazing man created the Emilio Nares Foundation in the memory of his young son who had died of cancer. Its Ride with Emilio program provides a vital service, transporting sick children whose families lack access to transportation to their cancer treatments and medical appointments. As we stood for the national anthem, Richard and I shared a moving embrace when we both saw a big yellow butterfly softly landing on a baseball player's cap. Always look for a sign!

* * *

While Mariah's Challenge was still a fledging nonprofit with limited resources, the 2009 New York Marathon was a high point. Traci O'Neill directed our enrollment and single-handedly worked on attracting participants. Due to a leg injury, I did not run with those great good souls, but I followed diligently the ones who did. They trained, searched for sponsorships, and still met hearth and home responsibilities: the essence of Butte Tough. As I followed along on the marathoners' website, tears flowed when my cell phone lit up with texts of successful completion. Mariah's Challenge Angel shirts were prominent in the crowd among the many thousands.

I did complete the 2010 New York Marathon along with Jenna and her friend Kati Thom. During some tough points in the race, the runners amazed me with their determination and concern for our youth. Their internal fortitude carried me along, but Jenna was my secret weapon, giving me a much-needed boost throughout. My lips still tremble in pride remembering her crossing the finish line.

In 2011, I completed the Chicago Marathon with Jim Cleary, who beat me to the finish line by at least an hour! Jim is another unintended member of the DUI-related death club. He ran in memory of his beautiful daughter Taylor, killed along with Ashlee Paternaude by a drunk driver talking on his cell phone in East Missoula.

Conversing with co-presenters at public events helped to ground me. The buildup to a presentation can be a soul heartache, nervousness at speaking before a crowd causing the body to shake internally without visible signs, even as involuntary muscles stiffen and lose cranial direction, muscles weakening with each step toward the podium. Senses are heightened, and I always have to beat back a boiling in my blood as I am transported back to that autumn night on October 27, 2007. When I am introduced, the world seems to stand motionless; transitioning back to real time, I am often impressed by the quietness of the hall or gym as I silently pray that one youth will listen and open their mind to the challenge at hand.

Each community or school event came with underlying ills and worries of its own. Counselors, teachers, and law enforcement officers were united in opposition to underage drinking and drinking, regardless of population size or geographical placement.

One October Night

* * *

What happened next was both unexpected and unbelievable. But it happened, and it thrust our movement into the national spotlight. Unbeknownst to me, my lovely daughter Jenna nominated me for the CNN Heroes program. I remember as if it was a moment ago Jenna's fingers hitting her laptop's keys, almost like she was playing a melody, and how after she stopped and closed the lid, I asked, "What were you doing, Bobenna?" (That's my nickname for her.) Her calm and confident reply humbled me: "I just submitted your name for the CNN Heroes award."

Jenna's soulful communication style must have strummed someone's heartstrings, because months later I received a call from CNN. My first reaction was that I was being punked! After my defensive reflex subsided, a woman with a calm, reassuring voice told me she was following up on Jenna's application. The world closed in just a bit as I went through a series of detailed questions about our Foundation, its tenets, and the overall scholarship process. The following three calls were increasingly detailed. Then, when I was selected to be one of 20 CNN Heroes globally, the life-altering experience of the Top 10 CNN Heroes selection process began.

The next step saw me interviewed in depth several times by the great good soul Lan Trinh, who along with an assistant flew in from New York to do a video segment on our work. Lan polished this rusty crowbar and somehow made me look presentable. Her story was titled "Grieving father offers teens money not to drink." I have no doubt she was responsible for keeping me in the running.

We could not have made it through this stage without Jimm Kilmer and Mary Garcia of Mining City Taxi and Pioneer Concrete, East Junior High Principal Larry Driscoll and his upstanding students, and Mariah's Challenge scholarship recipient Josh Panasuk. Butte High School also pitched in by allowing CNN to film a portion of the graduation ceremony.

Several months passed. Then I received a call from Hal German, the extraordinary senior producer of the CNN Heroes program. I had known generally, courtesy of Anderson Cooper, who made periodic announcements on his show, that the decisions were imminent. So when Hal called, I naturally thought he was calling the non-qualifiers before making the Top 10 calls.

Hal asked if I was sitting down, and I immediately stood up. The silence of a few seconds seemed like eternity. Next, he made it crystal clear that I could only divulge what he was about to reveal to one person, my wife. When, after congratulating me

Hitting the Road

on Jenna's application, Hal told me I had made the Top 10 class of 2012, I slammed back down in my chair. Overwhelmed, I thought of Jenna and her belief in me, and of Janice's smiling eyes. That moment is a memory that will not soon fade. The honor is a credit and tribute to Butte and the yearning of our youth for change.

Eyes flooded, I experienced a slow emotional shake throughout my body, and could barely register Hal's words of generous praise and his stern reminder that other than Janice I could tell no one, not my amazing board of directors, nor even Jenna. (The do-not-disclose injunction would prove tormenting, especially as to Jenna, whose application had made it all possible!) Hal elaborated further: if an independent news organization reported the information, I and Mariah's Challenge would be disqualified. I called Janice and told her of the extreme restrictions. Later that night, I had trouble looking Jenna in the eye.

As we waited for Anderson Cooper's official announcement, Janice and I had to deflect inquiries and quickly change the conversation when the subject came up. Thankfully, that announcement came a few days later, at which point the world started spinning even faster, starting with a Top 10 video segment. Rachel Grady of Loki Films was the maestro; she and her crew worked relentlessly. A presentation in Boulder at Jefferson High let them to see our movement in motion, including the effects of Jimm's and my presentations. The filming benefited from the talents and skills of Melissa Reynolds of Mkate Photography. Jon Wick also came through. And as the logistics of travel to California loomed, Montana Tech's Jedediah Wilson contributed his computer wizardry.

* * *

The CNN Top 10 awards were presented in Los Angeles at Shrine Auditorium. Janice, Jenna, and I flew in a few days beforehand. As I got to know the other nine nominees, I was impressed and then some at their accomplishments. For all of us, the daily schedule was tight, and I was thankful to have Janice and Jenna to tether me to the ground amid all the excitement. Day by day my appreciation of the determined spirits who worked for CNN grew exponentially: they made everything look easy. I also was able to meet past Heroes. Taryn Davis and Derreck Kayongo exhibited confidence and humility at the same time; their sheer humanity was intoxicating.

The evening of the awards was surreal. In the packed auditorium I recognized faces from TV and the movies. Then the ceremony began with a red carpet walk set in motion when I found three pennies strategically placed in my vision, which I took as a sign, an affirmation that the whole experience was fueled equally by love, pain, and forgiveness. Forgiveness is in itself a language of the soul. The grammar and syntax of grief and abject pain had written a novel within me, teaching that hate was not healing but only held me back from living and loving. But even with that knowledge, forgiving Mariah's murderer took time. And more so because he has never asked my forgiveness. To this day, I doubt he realizes the monumental consequences of his actions. He blamed everyone but himself. Certainly not his criminal misuse of alcohol.

My award was presented by the actor Josh Duhamel, whose heartthrob status no doubt had women listening intently as I thanked him. I made it through my short speech and welcomed Jenna and Janice's hugs and kisses. Walking to the picture-taking area, I had a chance to speak with Josh, who is a regular guy and father with Montana roots. I told him I had run a marathon with his then-wife. He cocked his head to the side and smiled. "You know who my wife is?" I said, "Yes, Fergie, from the Black Eyed Peas." During the 2011 Chicago Marathon, I told him, for the final five miles my iPod was stuck in a loop playing "I Gotta Feeling."

The votes were tallied and my friend Pushpa Basnet was selected as 2012's Top Hero. Her work with Nepal's forgotten and discarded children has given hope to an entire rising generation.

The after-party was a low-key affair. Several of the presenters attended, and the overall feeling was similar to a backyard barbeque. My memory of it is fuzzy, probably due to adrenaline and relief from not breaking down during the presentation. I do remember being in awe of U.S. Olympic swimmer Cullen Andrew Jones, and briefly holding his gold medal. (Jones was part of America's 4X 100 meter freestyle team at the 2008 Olympics in Beijing.) At the awards ceremony, he had presented Wanda Butts, one of my fellow Top 10 Heroes. In 2007 Wanda founded the Josh Project, in memory of her teenage son who never had a swimming lesson, and drowned. The Josh Project's mission is to provide children with swimming lessons and water safety education.

That evening I was able to thank Wallis Annenberg for her good works. Under her stewardship the Annenberg Foundation has supported educational and arts programs ranging in focus from the environment to social justice to animal welfare. The next day, the 2011 and 2012 Top 10 classes attended the Annenberg Alchemy, a grant assistance workshop for nonprofits where I learned ways to maximize the effectiveness of a board of directors. It was also an opportunity to say goodbye to new friends and peers.

Then it was home to Butte, reenergized to continue the mission of Mariah's Challenge.

Memorial site

Billboard

Right: Pete Sorini, guest speaker at Tip's (Teens in Partership)

Below: Mariah's Challenge basketball team

*Leo and Janice with Sen. Barack Obama,
the presumptive Democratic presidential nominee 07/04/2008 Butte, MT*

*Leo and Janice with Michele Obama,
wife the presumptive Democratic presidential nominee 07/04/2008 Butte, MT*

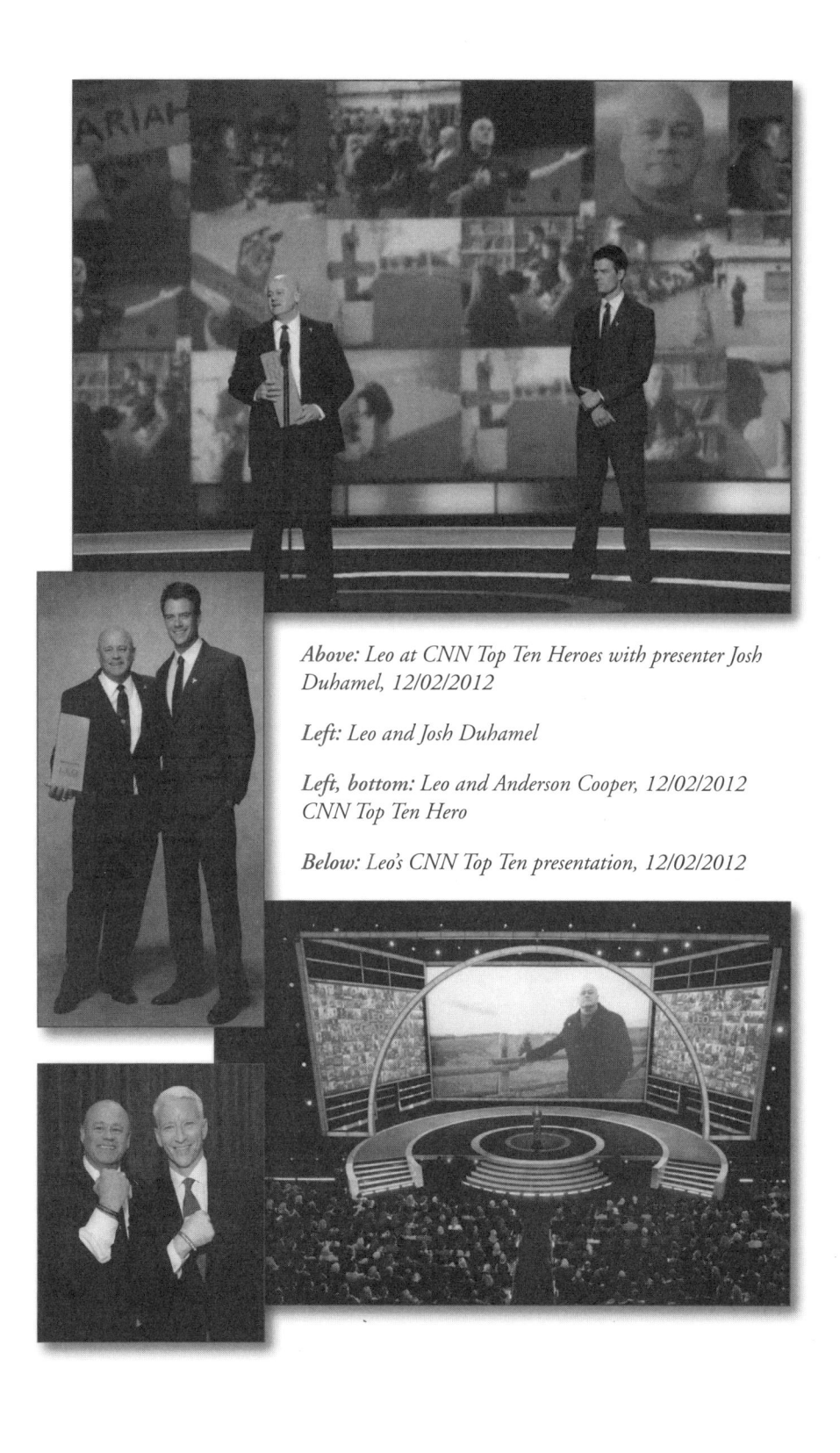

Above: Leo at CNN Top Ten Heroes with presenter Josh Duhamel, 12/02/2012

Left: Leo and Josh Duhamel

Left, bottom: Leo and Anderson Cooper, 12/02/2012 CNN Top Ten Hero

Below: Leo's CNN Top Ten presentation, 12/02/2012

Above: Bill Foley, Mariah's Challenge Half Marathon, 09/18/2016, Butte, MT

Left: Bradley Wilson, US Olympic Ski team member

Tatum and Tanner Eagan with license plates. Good friend of Leo's.

Above: Mariah's Challenge Scholarship Coin

Right: Governor Steve Bullock, Mariah's Challenge Awards guest speaker, 2017

2018 group picture from 2018 Mariah's Challenge Awards. Pictured: Ron Davis, emcee, owner of KBOW radio; Janice; Leo; Colt Anderson, UM Grizzly Football star and then current NFL specialist star, Minnesota Vikings, Philadelphia Eagles, Buffalo Bills, Indianapolis Colts; Jimm Kilmer; and Tim Rademacher

Below: Ed Rademacher, Mariah's buddy and grandfather, walking in the Mariah's Challenge 5k, 09/20/2015

Above: MT Tech football alumni, Pig Bowl and Mariah's Challenge golf organizer, Travis Hettick, and Leo at Fairmont Hot Springs Resort Golf Course

Seven Bridges teacher Brian O'Connor and Chappaqua, NY, Horace Greeley High School student at Mariah's Challenge presentation, 2019

Right: Mariah's family picture, head shot, 2007

Below: Mariah's poem. It is on the reverse side of her tombstone, now

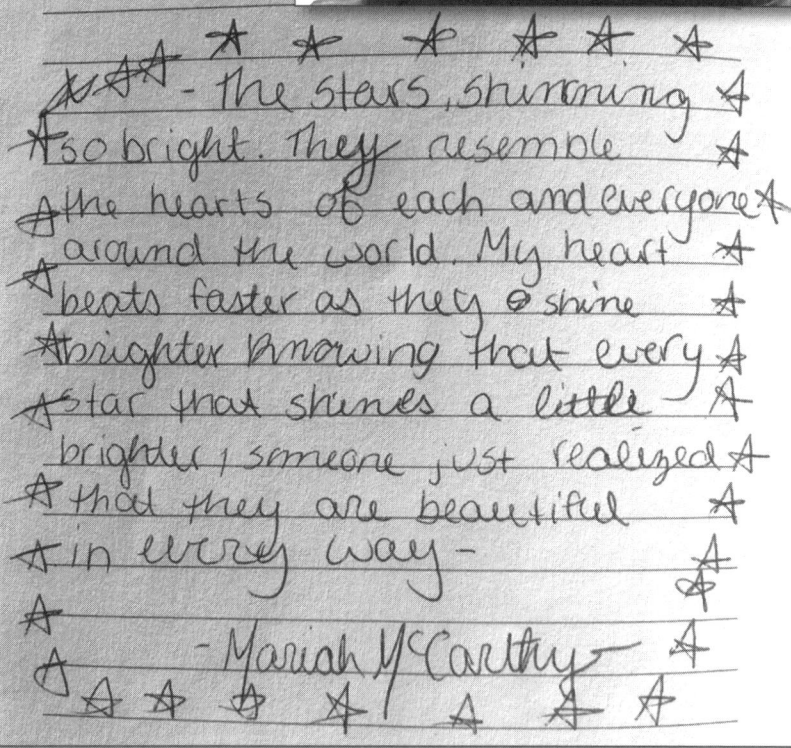

— The stars, shimmering so bright. They resemble the hearts of each and everyone around the world. My heart beats faster as they shine brighter knowing that every star that shines a little brighter, someone just realized that they are beautiful in every way —

— Mariah McCarthy

My friend Edwin Dobb, who died in 2019, wrote about Butte in publications ranging from the local to the national. Born here, Ed left in his late teens, only to return for another seventeen years as an adult. In a talk hosted by the Montana Historical Society, he shone a light on the "Romance of Butte," its "relentless self-mythologizing." Still, he was not immune to its allure, the hold Butte has on so many of us:

"In the brute actuality of the mining landscape, the industrial ruins, I see a kind of beauty—the beauty of unashamed candor. No sentimentality. No pretensions. No excuses. Yes, many of my neighbors, godblessem, do a remarkably effective job of blinding themselves to aspects of the town that don't accord with the stories they tell themselves and others, the stories that, paradoxically, have contributed much to the Mining City's vitality and longevity. This is a place, we must remember, that's gone to hell and back. And more than once."

In the aftermath of Mariah's death, we went to hell and back. Speaking for myself, coming out on the other side of grief was made possible through public service.

14

LOSS, PAIN, AND GRATITUDE

We miss Mariah so much. I know she would want us to live, to think of the good days and remember that the bad days were never quite so bad. And that she would not want us to carry hate in our hearts. Instead, we try to make the world a better place in her name and memory.

I have always been a reader of what are commonly called "self-help" or "inspirational" books, and after Mariah's death I found solace and wisdom—and sometimes the strength to continue—in the words and experiences of others. From my readings, reflections, and roller coaster of emotional states since Mariah's untimely death, I can only write about it from the heart.

We all have our moments of despair. Steven Pressfield has defined this emotional exhaustion as the All Is Lost moment, when we are faced with the decision whether to go on. Rocky as he leaves the arena. Players on the opposing team's turf who see a fearsome display of the home team's trophies and upscale weight room that puts their own modest facilities in the shade. My lowest point came after the return trip from Missoula, after stopping by the crime site late on Sunday, early Monday. The arena was our downstairs family room. Seeing Jenna watching *The Lion King*, a video I had seen with her and Mariah too many times to count, I snuggled up to the bottom of the couch, asking for permission from Jenna and silently screaming.

My first soul attack. My very being stopped. My nerves would not work, muscles turned to jelly, eyes gone blind but still making out images. I tried to move, to breathe, to even think. Some could say it was an anxiety attack, but I believe it was a soul's response to the spiritual battle I was going through.

God is asked many questions. Parents who leave the arena spiritually bloody and emotionally beaten up ask one question: Why? As my good friend Lonnie once told me, "Why is the hardest letter in life's alphabet." As I lay there on the couch next to Jenna, having hit bottom, I slowly raised my wracked shell of a body and barely mustered the words *I love you* to her. I knew I would survive, and that it would not be easy.

After loss, comes pain and grief. Grief is a construct of the mind. Those who have not experienced it firsthand sometimes relax their empathy. Others, who have been on the battlefield of grief, know that we all wear the garments of who we are and where we come from, and that grief is the All Pro on that battlefield. Grief has been iced up, stretched out, and taped up for battle—and suited for complete dominance.

The emotional pain is as real as physical distress, and surfaces on holidays and special events, in quiet rooms where only dust falls and songs having heartbreaking meanings. Our first Christmas as three was tough. Mariah was a holiday decorator. She would start many months before the thirty-day time frame started. If she worked at Macy's, the windows would be ready by October. I had to hold on to many memories to allow me just to breathe.

In a fairy tale, Rumpelstiltskin spun field hay into gold. History's foibles and follies record mankind's vain attempts to change one substance to another through alchemy, the attempt to find the ingredients, the chants, the right time of day to make gold out of base metals. In my case, the base metal was grief, and it came from everywhere. Small things, and big.

As I look out of my window and reminisce, I feel waves of emotion, ragged as they come, soothing as they leave: Mariah's smile with a missing tooth, her smile as a teenager just past her thirteenth birthday, and her smile after having her braces off. Her angelic smile. Memories of little Jenna and Mariah—pigtails on Mariah, beautiful curls on Jenna that only her mother could make. Coming home after a long day as a new insurance agent, and both of them screaming and jumping into my arms, saying "I love you, Dad!"—only a father knows how that feels.

Grief, as I came to learn, contains a small narcotic that can help you falsely protect yourself from life, but one that has no magic or alchemy. Especially when your grief is the result of the actions of another, in our case a reckless criminal, the temptation is strong to form the habit of hate. What I also learned is that grief loves sin, and can make you make you feel inferior for not wearing the supercharged "S" on your chest. It can make the simplest thought a zeppelin-sized heartache. It can belittle you for not standing up to it, and make you think the sin, the event changer, is your last stand, your walk uphill to Calvary. This is a necessary step, but not a place to get stuck.

At times you will find yourself feeling hatred, the galaxies of pain and ugliness, the torment of comets that sear the soul and take you to a new frontier of vengeance. You will despise everything about the criminal: his ancestry, his family, the torches of disgust they carry. You will not want to be around the expelled air from those insensitive lungs that propel the walking mannequin whose banality of pain does not even register the harm he has done, the pain he has caused others.

Hate is easier than grief. Inevitably, the wish for vengeance will arise. I don't mean killing or death; rather, a senseless mental wandering through avenues of disgust and anger. One target exists. The target wanders too, not solitary but an endless circus air-gun duck target. But vengeance gives liquid a stale taste, and food becomes a sponge, mastication without regard for what is being chewed. The body is on heightened alert, DEFCON 5 without the preparation or the hope that it is all a drill. No quarter is given. Ultimately, though, the longing for vengeance erodes stature, crumples lessons of propriety, and dissolves kindness.

As arguably humanity's second most powerful emotion—behind only that of love—anger, as opposed to vengeance, doesn't receive the appreciation and understanding it deserves. (Hate and vengeance, both stages in the process of grief, are fueled by anger, which needs time and requires effort to burn off.) Unfortunately, anger has a bad reputation and is seen as an emotion of evil. This couldn't be any further from the truth. There is no such thing as a good or evil emotion.

In *V!VA: Tools for Well-Being*, Katarina Gaborova terms anger "powerful and motivating." It may "be perceived as an emotion of helplessness, when in fact it can enable us to move forward and resolve our difficulties." Without it, says Donovan Westhaver, "we would essentially become a senseless society that acts indiscriminately without much of any purpose." While it is true that an angry wild man is buried deep within the soul of every good man, according to Gaborova anger can be "an important component of justice and fairness."

The key is knowing when and how to release anger by understanding selfishness, and when and how to keep anger guarded with the help of guilt and shame. Without our learning how to harness anger, chaos would become natural to us. Anger doesn't breed chaos; it is the dismissal of anger, guilt, and shame that often allows chaos to spread like a wildfire.

Faith, too, has an all-important part to play. Faith will tackle the remnants of sick desire of falsehood and lame excuses. It suffocates the struggling rationalizations of self-preservation. The battlefield is swiftly aerated anew with faint smells of the brave resolve of a new day. Yes, grief will persist, but it is not a militant way of life. When eviscerating denial and salving the wound with acceptance, when wrapped in the white linen of understanding, it is a positive. Convalescing is necessary as faith brings grief into proper alignment.

Working through the stages of grief and anger takes time and a lot of it, before you realize that forgiveness is not capitulation. Not at all. I learned that at my own pace, and eventually was able to forge ahead. Grief melts away as you embrace love, as you learn to accept what has happened and continue to see the best in yourself and others.

When gratitude comes, it does not boast over the prostrated body of grief; it holds a hand out to help. Gratitude is a willing sensei: gratitude for what persists, for people you love, for life itself, and for the memories of the dead. It rids ghouls of grief like boiling hot water cascading from a steaming teapot melting onto a sunless frozen back step of a poor man's home. When I am low, my belief that Mariah is near, closer than a breath of fresh air, helps me crawl out of the dark, dry, foul-smelling pit. Beware dark pit: your prey is not allowing you to stalk me, not today at least.

To me, grief and its adversary, gratitude, are like furniture; chairs mostly. You sit in your comfy chair, feeling the softness and kindness the fabric and stuffing gives your body. You sit and feel the common sensations of regret, pain, what if, anger, blind silent rage. You sit easy, no other levels of thinking. A slumber of silent screaming medicates you to a dull, numb, breathing, seething soul-heat.

But you need to look around for another seat, or else the cold, numbing shadow of grief and its posse of anger will lull you into a small world of mirrors and regret. You look and see other chairs. Finely built, with aesthetic value, welcoming. You struggle to place both hands on the slimy, sticky chair of grief, and you muster a short burst of strength and emotionally thrust yourself upwards. You stand. Light-headed, soul sweating, you catch your breath and step forward, Mind hazy with hate, you fumble and stumble towards the new chair. Twisting as you step, you bumble into it.

Then you look around with wide eyes and check your body, as your heart slows from a raging bull in your chest to a small rumble. It feels different, and you are not sure if this is better—but the view is definitely different. The sunlight peeping through semi-closed curtains is strong, like a child's gaze fixed on confections behind the counter at a candy store. Oddly, you notice the angles of other artifacts in the room. Pictures look different, memories are glazed with smiles, and pain is cooked away by slow, simmering acceptance. Love, our enduring angel of existence, presses on your cheek and the corners of your mouth crease upwards. Muscles, frozen like discarded snow banks, begin to melt. The agonizing pressure of the heart releases the chest to inhale without searing air.

Loss, Pain, and Gratitude

From your vantage point in this new chair, the world looks new. Air feels cold, but it is soothing like a midsummer Maui rainstorm. The air blankets you but is not suffocating or irritating.

The "you" above is of course me. Having worked the slow and painful steps of my emotions, I arrived at gratitude and shed tears of energizing relief. I am a puddle in the much-sought oasis of optimism and love.

My father, Dan McCarthy, always said the reason the Irish are such ferocious fighters is that they were never taught to run. He was a well-known boxer and fighter through his teens and in college, then in the army. I was not as tough as him, but I could take a punch.

My favorite philosopher is Seneca, who somehow, in words written thousands of years ago, conveys my feelings about my heritage, and about Butte, the only home on this earth Mariah ever knew:

"No prizefighter can go with high spirits into the strife if he has never been beaten black and blue; the only contestant who can confidently enter the lists is the man who has seen his own blood, who has felt his teeth rattle beneath his opponent's fist, who has been tripped and felt the full force of his adversary's charge, who has been downed in body but not in spirit, one who, as often as he falls, rises again with greater defiance than ever."

15

FRÉAMHACHA AGUS BRAINSÍ

*S*t. Patrick's Day may have a little parade in New York City, but we celebrate it in style in Butte. When the girls were small, Janice decorated the house several weeks prior, as a result of insistent requests from the two wee fans of the holiday. We would bring them to the annual parade, to be followed up at home with Janice's incomparable corn beef and cabbage.

When you grow up with my last name, no one is unaware you come from Irish stock. And when you share a first name with thirteen popes, it's a safe bet your family is Catholic. As a young boy going to Catholic school, never in my wildest dreams did I see myself as a writer, and never in my worst nightmares did I see myself writing this book. We never know what life has in store, and my life, which has been blessed in so many ways, has been indelibly defined by the death of my youngest daughter at the age of fourteen by an underage drunk driver.

Mariah Daye McCarthy was uncommonly proud of her Irish heritage. I can recall, soon after her birth, holding her and softly singing an Irish lullaby, whispering to her that I would always protect her. Nor will I ever forget, in another hospital room, on the evening of her death, singing an Irish lullaby through tears that would not stop into her asphalt-scarred ear. When I sang to both of my girls in the St. James delivery room, I never imagined the tune would become a farewell lullaby.

Along with Jenna, Mariah shared her Irish pride with countless other Butte natives who trace their lineage back several generations, and before that to the Emerald Isle itself. Butte patriots tend to be blessed (some would say cursed too) with a double-barreled pride: in our hometown and in our Irishness. The McCarthys plead guilty as charged!

When Mariah was hit by a truck near midnight on October 27, 2007, our family already had plans for a trip to Ireland the following the summer, to explore our roots and meet some members of the family. That trip never took place, and has not taken place to this day, though we all hope that someday it will.

Janice and I both have deep roots in Ireland and elsewhere. My paternal side can be traced to Murtagh McCarthy of Rohane, County Cork. Through marriage with the O'Sullivan and Spillane Clans, the tree started to grow and branched out across the ocean to Boston, then to Ishpeming, an iron ore mining town in the Upper Peninsula of Michigan, and Virginia City, Nevada, before the McCarthy Clan reached Butte, where we were known for athletics, boxing skills in particular.

Some of the men worked the mines; others, along with their sisters and wives, labored aboveground. Putting food on the table was more the priority than education, and typically it was the children of miners who graduated high school. My father and his brother Bill were the first to graduate college, at Columbia University (since renamed University of Portland). And for many, many years, my Uncle Jack was Butte's fire chief.

On my mother's side, paternal roots spread to the township of Cotton, part of Switzerland County, Indiana, with the Theo Buchanan Clan, and then to Utah before coming to Butte. My mother's father, Albert Forrest, who was from Idaho Springs, Colorado, died young. My grandmother, Pearl, better known as Da, then married a colorful character called Alvin "Bunny" Shea, whose unique nickname came from his job as a hoist operator for the Anaconda Copper Mining Company. He was in charge of lowering the miners to the dark and accident-prone depths of Butte's mines. Bunny came by his nickname on the job, when a mouthy Welsh miner made a disparaging comment on his age and the lack of perceived strength it required to control the brake systems of the hydraulics. Bunny proceeded to release the cage at full speed and deftly apply the brakes yards away from the bottom of the dirt and wooden shaft. At the end of the shift in the earth's bowels, the young man made it known not to insult the hoist operator or he "will bounce you like a bunny at the bottom." A nickname earned with full respect.

Pearl (Da) ran a local grocery store in the neighborhood of Centerville; it became a place of conversation and a meeting spot during many miner strikes in Butte. Her kindness was a common trait in many neighborhoods and stores during lean times and famine.

My father, Dan, was the oldest of six. His siblings were Bill, Mary, Delores, Dorothy, and Jack. A close family, they depended on each other for support in fighting bullies. Together they picked up loose coal dropped from railroad cars, to sell and give the proceeds to their mother. Hand-me-down clothing was the order of the day; passing on new shoes from older to younger brothers was a hint of my father's heart and love. He worked for the State of Montana and served a term as a State Representative, going on to become payroll specialist for Anaconda Copper. All this came after his service in World War II, where he was an army medical specialist on the USS *Mercy* in the South Pacific. He returned home to make a life and start a family, with my mother, Gertrude Veronica Shea.

Our family grew to eleven children, including Robert, from my mother's earlier grim union to a wife-beating bastard. Robert died young but was always included in our prayers; my father treated his memory as his own. As the youngest of the brood, I had many role models when it came to toughness, character, and heart. My brothers Dan, Dinty, Mark, and Steve were like giants to me growing up. My brother Michael died in infancy. My lovely sisters bore the names Suki, Toni, Meg, and Deb. I was lucky to have so many siblings helping and telling me the errors of my ways!

Janice was born a Rademacher, with paternal roots sprouting from County Cork. Her grandfather moved from Germany to Minnesota, and then to Montana, while her sturdy grandmother, Hanorah Hanley, left Berehaven, Cork, and rode the Atlantic waves upon the Compania passenger ship.

On the maternal side, Janice's family tree started on one side from Berehaven, County Cork, then intertwined with the Janhunens (Otto Anton and Hilda Myyra), who hailed, respectively from Helsinki and Vipuri. The McFadden line followed the Irish miners to Butte. Otto and Margaret McFadden branched out with William (Jinx), Peggy, James (Gus), Patty, and Dan. Patty married Ed Rademacher, and they filled a house with quality children—Ed, Susan, Julie Ann, Janice, Tim, Karen, and Dan.

Janice briefly introduced herself earlier in these pages. Here, she picks up her story: "My life growing up was one of Butte people working hard from eight to five, with love and concern after dinner. Chores and daily home duties were a norm, as was the time to relax when all obligations were completed. My brothers and sisters and I grew up in a supportive atmosphere. Intra-sibling squabbles and competition were on the ice rinks and we could all tease effectively. Friends and great memories of this time in life always remain a part of you, like the rising and setting of the sun. Our extended family, cousins and in-laws, were a big part of our lives. Family is the rock we leaned on during celebrations and funerals and other times of need.

"We grew up in a supportive environment and were encouraged to work while in school, if we were not playing sports. Growing up here, being part of the history and culture, gives you much to be proud off and some not to be. In my family, alcohol was not an issue. My parents raised us to have a healthy respect for drinking responsibly, if at all. They themselves do not drink."

As have many other boys, I grew up on the streets of Walkerville and Centerville and was raised in the back alleys of Butte. My hometown has a special taste of character and flavor of attitude. It can be felt in the family-owned restaurants and backyard barbeques, which serve food ranging from ethnic dishes to specialized offerings that would tempt the palettes of a globe-trotting gourmand.

Butte, Montana, is known internationally as the one-time home of gold and silver prospectors and mining camps, a no-holds-barred city that in its heyday had up to a hundred thousand citizens. Early on, BUTTE TOUGH became our unofficial motto, and for abundant reason. We come from hardy stock, miners who pick-axed the earth to line the pockets of Copper Kings. Miners who rubbed shoulders with men and women engaged in other back-breaking occupations and in service-related fields, in stores whose owners needed hard negotiating skills and big hearts. A miner could rise from the steamy, muddy bowels of the earth, quickly shower, then plant himself at his corner or neighborhood bar to imbibe his fill of whiskey and beer.

The phrase also applies to men and women from the 59701 zip code with storied careers in the military, the arts, and sports, including coaches at the college and professional levels; a long list of natives that could be longer still: Evel Knievel, Keith Sayers, Colt Anderson, Tim Montana, Rob O'Neill, Brad and Bryon Wilson, Edwin Dobb, Pete Sorini, Paul Dennehy, Krystal Carlson, Rob and Kelly Johnson, Anna Fabitz, Judy Morstein Martz, Shirley Penaluna Shea, Shawna Hanley, Paul Dennehy, Mike Mansfield, Pat Williams, Brian Morris, John Banovich, Rose Hum Lee, Sonny Lubick, Jim Sweeney, Pat Ogrin, Erin Popovich, and Darrell Turley.

Butte Tough has many definitions and no exclusive ethnic ties. One definition, historically, has been misplaced pride in drinking, and starting underage, and in driving under the influence. But we are working to replace that connotation, so it means, instead, high scholastic marks and not consuming alcohol underage or doing drugs.

The essence of Butte Tough is what is in your heart and soul. It means being unbowed even when you are bloodied; it means getting up to help your fellow human being.

* * *

Coming of age, I held a range of jobs, starting in high school, to save for college. Working summers with the early morning sidewalk crew at the County Public Works, I got to learn to enjoy working a jackhammer—if the word "enjoy" can be used in relation to a jackhammer. This job instilled in me a deep sense of respect for those hardy men and women who labor to bring food to their family's table and for the financial health of their children's future.

Graduating high school, I went to MSU in Bozeman, where I squandered the learning options afforded to me. Too much fun—and not at the library. But I was lucky to continue my scholastic adventures at Western Montana College, in Dillon, while working as a bartender/bouncer at a local bar called Papa T's during the week and at the Vu Villa Bar in Butte on weekends. As was true at MSU, at Western I didn't crowd the top percentage with my grades, but I did graduate, with a Social Studies Broadfield degree, and ventured out hoping to find work as a teacher/coach.

After stints as a substitute teacher and a bartender, I was hired by the Butte Pre-Release Program, run by Mike Thatcher, which gave me insight into the rehabilitation and counseling of convicted felons. The good people there taught me that a second chance at life is what our country is about, a second chance dependent on the sincere desire to change.

My next position was with Rivendell helping Butte's youth and teens who struggle with behavior-related issues compounded with drug and sexual abuse history. The in-house facility showed me how fragile our souls are, especially when confronted with troubled family and social situations. The determined work there by floor counselors and aides, nurses, and therapists makes a difference.

Life-changingly, I met Janice Rademacher through a friend and relative, Dave, shortly after graduating from Butte Central. A Butte High graduate, Janice was an active member of the Butte High Purple B's, a group that entertained halftime crowds at the East Junior High football stadium and during basketball games. She excelled at this strenuous extracurricular activity not unlike other sports and was selected as the Top B of the Year! (I was lucky we never met in high school. If we had I would still be single!)

We dated, we broke up, and we got back to together, much to my benefit. Then we became husband and wife. Becoming a husband was a hands-on learning apprenticeship. No amount of watching *Father Knows Best* and John Wayne movies prepared me for it. Not to mention that my own father, a survivor of the Great Depression and World War II, didn't have an extensive library of How To or personal development books around the house. After ten children he must've hoped his eleventh born would absorb such matters through observation and osmosis.

Parenting is an experience of the senses that takes the optimism of a hard-rock miner and the patience of a rancher. I stumbled and fumbled many times, only to be looked at with the loving and forgiving eyes of Janice and little Dublin and Cork, my early nicknames for Jenna and Mariah. The self-centeredness of youth quickly dissipates when you realize you are the reason for grub on a plate.

I'm not the first to realize that fact, nor will I be last. Yes, long days at the office produced self-induced stress, but it was immediately vaporized when my two wee folks met me at the door. Wrestling on the ground with them, using my bent knees as a slide and stifling laughs, I listened to them tell me about the seriousness of *their* day.

No doubt I graded out as a low B student, but I was a valedictorian when it came to love and appreciation of my family. My life of gratitude was always blended with dreams of health and happiness and whispered hopes of a future when both daughters had finished college and found their self-directed bliss as I sat back and watched the completion of their soul's contentment, the doddering father dispensing unwanted and outdated sage advice. A drunken youth took that away from me.

* * *

A common American story is of wanting to leave your hometown, often to think of it as an escape. Even as a young boy, I never wanted to live anywhere but Butte. Did I think I would end up as a State Farm Insurance Agent? Well, no, but I did, and I love being one. It is my career.

That career started when I was hired as an auto claim representative. Supportive management and dedicated peers helped show me the ropes of my new profession. For seven years I worked as a claims adjuster with reputable attorneys, many of whom became my friends. Insurance may seem dry to an outsider, but human drama, and yes, human tragedy, is an everyday occurrence when you are regularly called upon to summon empathy and sympathy, most especially when lives are lost or derailed by injuries. All of that training and experience has made me a better a State Farm Agent, a position I attained in 1996 when Don Ulrich retired, leaving big shoes to fill.

In the State Farm system, an agent runs his or her own agency and is the CEO, CFO, secretary, and snow shoveler. Although I am licensed to sell various kinds of insurance throughout Montana, my terrain is centered in Butte and the surrounding areas. Applications for insurance and inspection of property have been part of my daily rounds ever since opening the door on my first day as an agent, and every day is another opportunity to meet souls from diverse walks of life, souls with afflictions ranging from injuries to loss of life. And I still learn something new before I lock up for the night. In the past twenty-five years, I have employed many gracious workers and am thankful for the trust my clients have placed in me. Currently, I have a stellar staff of four.

When Mariah was murdered by vehicular manslaughter, among the grim tasks I had to complete were to see various auto, health, and life insurance claims through. No training ever prepares you to sign a death claim for your own daughter. Others may armchair the situation with unwanted advice, but to no avail.

* * *

Marriage, family, and building a business based on high-volume interaction with others has seen me push away outside activities not related to my business, peers, and family. (My family is the slave of this gash of self-dignity.) Personal acceptance is the cornerstone of any high-volume interaction. You push hard to help others, keep their interest foremost. And when money transactions are involved, especially in business, life can become a slave to your highs and lows.

In the wake of Mariah's death, when I was forced to confront local attitudes of denial and anger about the use and abuse of alcohol, I could not avoid looking at how inherited cultural attitudes toward drinking as a mark of manhood have papered over the devastation that alcohol abuse, both by the young and grown-ups, has caused in so many families including my own, historically, and up to the present. The tragic consequences for us, and the Okrusches and Kilmers, are the result of an underage driver's choice to drink and get behind the wheel. His choice made sure others will be forever changed. The McCarthy family now has a tombstone to visit and a life of What Ifs.

To reiterate, when I speak to youth groups on choices and behavior, I take pains to let them know that I do not hold myself up as a paragon of virtue. I am a work in progress, and try to be honest about my own failings, and to illustrate my talks with lessons gleaned from my past. Before I saw the light and assumed full responsibility as a man, husband, and father, I was a full-fledged initiate in this practice, and it caused many problems for me. My father also had issues with alcohol in his early years and throughout the Second World War and after. Many homes have similar stories to tell. ❧

Epilogue

We live in deeds, not years; in thoughts, not breaths;
In feelings, not in figures on a dial.
We should count time by heart-throbs. He most lives
Who thinks most, feels the noblest, acts the best.
And he whose heart beats quickest lives the longest:
Lives in one hour more than in years do some
Whose fat blood sleeps as it slips along their veins.
Life's but a means unto an end; that end,
Beginning, mean, and end to all things—God.
The dead have all the glory of the world.

-Philip James Bailey

OCTOBER 2020

Years have passed since we said goodbye to Mariah, though we still plan our annual Christmas morning breakfasts and dinners with four chairs but only three plates, and with quiet dust falling on our forever teenager's bedroom upstairs. When something as senseless as the death of your youngest daughter at the hands of another happens, you try to rebuild your world as best you can. As I was waiting for Mariah's body to be prepared for organ donation, in a quiet hallway of St. Pat's Hospital I came upon a sign quoting the French philosopher Voltaire: "Faith is believing when it is beyond the power of reason to believe." Mariah had faith—in her sister, in her mother and me, in her friends. I try to be worthy of that faith.

In my eulogy for Mariah, I thanked her and Jenna's friends for their beautiful memorials at the Immaculate Conception Church and on the wall on Blacktail Lane near where the bodies were left. And I spoke to them out of my own pain. "The pain you are experiencing," I said, "is pain of separation, pain of the unknown, pain of asking Why. I do not have the answers. Please talk with your loved ones. You can always talk to us. We might not have the answers, but we will have hugs and a shoulder to cry on." Mariah and Jenna's friends did not let us down. The best of Butte is not to be found underground; the people who walk on top of the mines are the best of Butte.

Epilogue

Mariah's Challenge was born from tragedy and took upon itself a mission of hard work to help youth through cultural change. The Foundation's success has not been a case of "I told you so," but rather one of "We knew it could be so." My belief in our youth and in the ability of people to grow has never been stronger.

By way of closing, let me address the young, with words that are as immediate to me today as they were in 2007:

Mariah's departure is defined in a message, a challenge, and a wish. The message is simple and direct: Don't Drink and Drive. It is against the law, but more importantly it is wrong. It is not a right, and the cycle of indifference and of winking in a "boys will be boys" way must be broken. Mariah's Challenge and Mariah's Wish are for you to be the first generation of youth from Butte to not drink until your twenty-first birthday. And not to drink and drive. Ever. Break the sick cycle, make a difference. Think, Take Action, Make MIP's (minors in possession) a thing of the past. If you do so and work with your school and the Butte Police Department, and do not get any MIP's during high school, the Mariah Daye McCarthy Scholarship will be there to help you with your college expenses.

Help this lonely club my family belongs to become one no other parent or family member can be inducted into. ❦

Additional Materials

The 10th annual Mariah's Challenge Scholarship Ceremony was held last Thursday in the Montana Tech auditorium and recognized 21 Butte seniors for their dedication to preventing underage drinking.

From article by Maddie Vincent, May 20, 2019, *Montana Standard*

Victim Impact Statement of Leo McCarthy

JANUARY 21, 2009

After a plea agreement was reached, one I was not happy with, I addressed the judge and the criminal directly. (His name has been removed, although it is a matter of public record.) I spoke from notes and my blood was boiling. The text below has been reconstructed from my notes and lightly edited—not to make me appear more articulate, but rather for clarity and length. The remarks represent my opinions only.

I want to thank the Honorable Judge Newman, City Attorneys B. McCarthy, M. Clauge, E. Joyce, and S. Cox, and Detectives Doug Conway and Ed Lester, and the Butte Police Department. Thank you for giving my family and me justified vengeance through the legal system. My family and I do not derive any soul sustenance or sense of well-being here today. No sort of equality of actions felt. No sense of completion. Our lives have not been the same since October 27, 2007.

I am a father of a murdered daughter, father of a grieving surviving sibling, husband to a mother who has mourned and still does for the death of her daughter. I am here to speak for the dead.

The dead that this table on my left cannot speak of. They speak of legal matters instead. This table cannot do so because the men at it tried for well over a year to say the dead never existed and [the criminal] did no wrong.

I'll use your parents' term—"compound"—when referring to your home since that is what I heard for two days. I won't have to dumb this down for you, since you are smarter than the oaf you try to present to the media. You play the dumb-kid-from-the-compound act very well. Hopefully, you don't go through any of your convenient blackout episodes.

It has taken 363 days for you to face me, 399 days for you to finally accept your 100 percent involvement. Within this time, you have been convinced or taught of your guilt that it does not matter and is someone else's fault. You have had holidays and birthdays. You still are hurting the victims by your actions.

Mariah has none, she is forever 14. Jenna will never have her best friend. Janice will never get to cook and prepare dinner with Mariah. I will never have my Christmas snowball fight with my daughters and nieces. We will never get to watch Mariah, Valarie, and Kaitlyn jump on the trampoline.

I will never be able to watch my daughters and their mother plan weddings. We will never see Mariah graduate from high school or college. We will never get to help her through life's trial and tribulations.

A person's worth to society is measured by the goodness he or she brings to others minus the bad. The bad can be lessened or diminished by the degree of accountability and acknowledgement in making the wrong right. It is a scale of one's soul, a measurement of how one is taught by his parents and the atmosphere of the family hearth and home.

You are most wanting in the scale of measurement of your soul, and are an intimate reflection of you, only. The killing of my daughter and the brutal injury to her friends was not helped by your cowardly actions or your thinking you had a right to drive drunk before you hit them, and as you came back to revel in your carnal construction of death. As you viewed your carnage, and as you failed to render aid, added to your subsequent spineless acts of covering up your actions—all of these prove to me a new definition of the banality of evil. I do not know of the personal conversations you have with your soul or if evil abides within your body, but your actions show your personality and the callous attitude you have toward life, and the accumulation of your education, and the values taught by the compound.

The banality of evil, to me, is the normalization of the unthinkable. You try to make unspeakable behavior seem okay. Normalizing your murderous act, normalizing your degrading actions immediately after and up to this date, with the support of the compound and your legal team, is sick and not morally right. To think that your reaction is sound and accepted and it is just the way it should be. No questions asked. You and the compound have rationalized that drinking beer after beer all night, driving your truck, killing and hurting is okay. It is normal behavior, just accept it. Rationalizing the unspeakable comes easy when money is used. It involves tactics that stall and delay the process. Using smoke and mirrors by retreating to feigned ignorance or planned acts of stupidity, or mysterious cases of blackout just cultivates this sickness. To me, it is like losing part of your soul as you try to continue to make yourself believe your own press releases of your lack of responsibility.

The psychosis of all of this is that you think you should not do any time in prison for your actions! Your actions, your faked story of blacking out, constitute the method of your organized and systematic way of saying you had a right to do what you did, and that March 12, 1993, when Mariah's was born, and October 28, 2007, her death date, mean nothing for you. Your jaded and dull response shows you have no remorse or the slightest bit of compassion. To lie, to not help, to run home and have mommy and daddy make everything better—these are the acts of a coward. The ugliest act of banality is when others' lives do not matter to you and people serve only as a tool or hindrance to your preservation.

I wonder what type and color of entity will pick you up on your last day here. I know what type picked up Mariah. Whatever picks you up, I hope it deposits you far away from Mariah.

What personal abuse engulfs your soul that you needed to medicate the ugliness by drinking an off-the-charts amount of beer before you jumped into your loaded weapon? What abuse of education or lack thereof from the compound allows you to drink so much? What abuse or sickness erupts from the compound culture to let you spit in the face of reality and in the grieving faces of families? What gave you the right to run home and try to not be held accountable just because you think a home is an island, a country unto itself? It isn't normal and the behavior should not be accepted, socially or legally.

You have been well taught or well trained in the last year to show no emotion, no acceptance, and no visible manifestation of your responsibility of your actions. This is a real credit to the compound culture and your dream team. Too bad the people you look to for moral guidance and a compass of integrity failed you as you failed yourself.

I wonder, if it was your counsels' relative or daughter, would they be so antiseptic about all of this. I know the sensitivity chip was removed or probably not installed, but to act callously and make comments of pride and disregard for the afflicted is disheartening. I hold commonality as a male of the species with you, your father, and your counsel, but nothing else.

One question: How would you feel if this murder was done to one of your family? Seeing how the family has reacted, I could surmise how vile and vindictive the response would be if I struck down one of the twins, acted indifferent and indignant, and essentially, through actions, said, "Just get over it." Or better, "I JUST hit a deer."

The sins of the son are sometimes not sins of the father, but I hold your parents responsible due to their intimate knowledge of your past behavior and lack of responsibility and respect for others that finally erupted on October 27, 2007.

The drinking age is 21 not 20, but I guess the drinking age is different for you. I guess with your rules of morality, if you drink and drive and get caught your punishment is that your truck is parked. Expressing your insensitivity on steroids. Your looks of indignation do not come from moral superiority, they come from fear and lack of integrity.

You must be rock stupid to think we would believe your story. You and your callous dream team called my daughter "just a deer." Your public relations team first had you as a resident of Helena and then strived to picture you as a resident and permission-giving resident of the compound. What an insult to the fine town of Helena, and a laudable display of genuine disregard of human life. Living on a steady diet of lack of responsibility, full of calories of disrespect and lack of integrity, is visible. You are obese from your appetite of having no integrity and having no empathy for my family's pain.

You're a bully. You lived the life of a bully, a life proud of drinking and making people less to you than they really are. Bullies always take cheap shots at people who are tougher and better than themselves. They take these shots from behind then run home to mommy and daddy with a fabrication of lies. Lies of falsehood that you had no involvement or you were nine miles away looking for deer. When caught, you cry and you run to mommy and daddy to protect you and to start writing checks to make everything better and to enable your lack of responsibility even further.

The only way you could have met those three beautiful girls is how you violently introduced yourself to them. You would have no other chance to be in their presence other than how you struck them. You are definitely a prince but the year is 2008, not the 1600s. If the prince hurts and kills, he must pay.

How do you hit deer on a walking path, or is the story that you were changing a CD? Or was it the street construction that made you lose control and hit them? Nothing that I have heard relates to your involvement or real acceptance other than a last ditch option in a porous defense. I know what happened and wish I could prove it. But I think only you, me, and Mariah know of it. You saw those three girls walking on the path and tried to scare them, and lost control. I don't want to think deeper of this anymore but I shudder if that is the case. I can't prove it, but I know that is how bullies operate. Cheap shot, run home, lie, have mommy and daddy enable you, and try to say the girls were on the street and they hit your truck.

You only show the right emotions when it concerns you or you might have your mug shot on TV or in the paper, not for others or their pain. I did see you show anger regarding your displeasure of a comment made contesting your innocence during the hearing, and your later laughter after a note was passed to you. It was an interesting show of sick hubris. I also saw your joviality with your friends in the rotunda during a break in proceedings. I guess you are just misunderstood and have personal problems of communication and only act in anger. The compound school system only teaches self-preservation and not kindness to others. You must have been the valedictorian.

I was also stunned to see your legal team congratulate themselves in front of the families for trying to eradicate the whole night of October 27, 2007, and I wonder what the counsel would do if it was one of their own flesh and blood killed. I could only imagine what recipe of pain would be made and dished out. Take all the poison fruit from the tree and then chop it down. If it was their daughter that was so violently murdered, would they be so detached, so aloof, so proud? I guess it is easy to be intellectually sympathetic when death doesn't knock on your door with beer breath.

Speaking as a father who has had the sacred ripped from his life, I saw no emotion from you as Detective Stanton's police vehicle DVD was played. You saw it twice, once with your legal bodyguards, the second standing by yourself, and you showed no emotion or hurt. You knew I was looking at you and standing less than seven feet away. You still ignored the results of your killing act. I guess the compound-issued excuse is you have problems showing your emotions. Your act has not fooled anyone and never will. Your tears of remorse are in direct proportion to your loss of freedom, not to the death of my daughter or the injuries to her two friends.

People say you hurt. I saw you hurt only because of what you finally had to admit. I saw your polarity and the reasoning of your hurt. Behind the pouty face of Little Boy Blue in the paper, you have showed to me what guides your emotions, your hurt. During the two-day circus display, I witnessed the killer of my daughter, his dream team and his parents, and the disregard for the life and death of my daughter of 14 years. Your support system tried to deny my daughter's existence. You have denied you murdered her with your truck. Your compound supporters deny she was on the walking path. Your dream team tried to deny she ever lived or was born on March 12, 1993. The lack of compassion seemed an outward display of indignation from having to go through the whole process.

I guess the shoes left on the path 110 feet away from where the three landed didn't matter. The three dents on the hood of your bully buggy Ford 150 were not enough proof. The blood wasn't deer blood, but of those three Butte gals you violently hit. To you, you drive drunk, to me it is attempted murder. No excuse that you were drunk, no excuse that you blacked out. You just did it.

You are a cold, calculating coward who knew what you did. But how could you hit three girls, black out, turn around your weapon, get out of the weapon, walk around, black out, run to Shane Ford, lie, black out, walk back to your weapon, black out, turn your truck around, black out because you see Shane giving CPR to a deer, go home, black out, and have a quality discussion with one of your parents about the day, minus the blackout sessions and your personal record of beer consumption at a party?

The leader of the compound said you were in shock. Shock from what? A mighty Elmer Fudd hunter like you goes in shock from seeing a dead deer? They know what you did, and so do you.

I find it interesting in your story to Officer Moore that you said he had the wrong guy and you hit a deer. How does one remember that you hit a deer and hit it out at Roosevelt Drive, after all of those tragic blackout episodes and the shock you were in? What did you really mean: Wrong guy?

Your whole story serves as a great pilot show for CSI: The Compound.

You killed her.

Something I really don't think you accept. As history repeats itself, you will have your attorneys read your statement. I wonder if your father will read it for you. If you are a man and try to read it without becoming a soggy Kleenex, I know you will tremble and cry and your public relations team will try to illustrate that you and the compound are the only victims, and you should have leniency.

Your daytime Emmy-winning act will be interesting to watch, if indeed you do perform the drama episode. The amount of tears and sobs are indirectly related to the loss of your freedom, not what you did on October 27 2007. You could crawl up Main Street to the Alice Pit, over broken glass, naked every day until you die, and it would not even be a starting point. I guess people should feel sorry for you since you weren't given a coat or the vehicle's heater wasn't turned on, or you weren't allowed to have your other boot put on.

Across the way, with the blinking strobe lights on, my daughter and her two friends were lying on cold asphalt with no shoes on and their skin exposed through ripped clothes. Mariah's exposed toes through her shredded socks were the only physical clues to her mother and sister that it was her being worked on.

You have had it easy from day one. You still have the privilege to drive, to work and to be with your friends. I really wonder if you quit drinking before you changed your plea on October 2, 2008. A plea so eloquently spoken for you in court by one person and another saying off-camera he would have gotten you off on all the charges. You have gotten to go home, have holidays, and have the system

Victim Impact Statement of Leo McCarthy

coddle and enable you without making you acknowledge your actions. The days of honoring your Peter Pan way of life and your hanging out with the Lost Boys in the drunken playground of Never Never Land will soon come to an end. Your faked or drug-induced emotional outpouring, your anxiety, your fears and tears are directly related to your loss of freedom, not for my family's pain. Too bad it will be the last statement heard in this court today.

We had to endure two days of experiencing the compound's personal investigation of distance and time.

Since the compound likes numbers, distances, and time frames, I thought you would like to hear some of ours.

Oh, Janice, Jenna, and I didn't have the luxury of your support system that made a mockery of the three families, as well as being indignant, but so callous as to not even acknowledge that Mariah lived and that Jenna, Kaitlyn, and Val were in the crowd at the two hearings.

We had to do the following because you made us do it. First, the numbers:

5262 days Mariah had lived on this earth.

29,200 days that you took from Mariah.

61 to possibly 181 days you will probably serve in jail for the death of Mariah, injury to Valarie, Kaitlyn, and lying until no nook was left in the rat hole at the compound.

Zero days that you will not be able to hunt once out of jail.

10 years that you will be able to hide and circumvent the system and go back to your compound way of life of drinking and partying, a life normalizing and accepting the unthinkable.

Now distances. Since the compound did your own time trials, I give you this:

325 feet from her front door (where Mariah was left for dead); the same distance Janice and Jenna walked down to the site; the same distance I have walked several times on lonely holiday nights.

50 feet, how far Mariah was violently ejected from her shoes.

4 miles from the site to St. James (travel time 5 minutes).

210 miles to Missoula by car, which took more than three hours, my family traveled in the early morning of October 28, 2007.

Less than a half a mile, how far you drove after almost hitting Shane Ford and Mariah, again.

210 miles in 38 minutes, to get Mariah to Missoula via Life Flight. You made it possible through the machines needed to keep her alive that no room was available for me to fly with her.

The unknown distance our life will be without Mariah. I wasn't ready to begin trying to remember her laugh, her smile, and the soft tone of her saying her own name. We will never hear the melody of her laughter or enjoy seeing her and Jenna watching their Sunday night video.

And since the compound did some time trials on their own, so did we:

SATURDAY, OCTOBER 27, 2007

11:45 P.M.: When you killed her. You were not changing a CD, you didn't hit a deer. The contour of the road didn't make you swerve; they were not on the street. You didn't black out. More excuses, more normalizing the wrong. You and I know what you were doing and why you were doing it.

11:50 TO 11:55: When you didn't take the opportunity to ask for help from those two great good people, Denise and Kevin Horne, as you saw those good citizens coming to their windows. You ran 15 yards to lie to one of the greatest Good Samaritans this town has, Shane Ford, that deer were hanging out on a walking path and you hit them. Or is the story the deer hit you? Do you know Shane gave us the opportunity to say goodbye to Mariah by his CPR?

SUNDAY, OCTOBER 28, 2007

12:04 A.M.: When dispatch got the call of your vehicular manslaughter.

12:10: When the site was full of medical personnel.

12:25 (approximately): When you probably used your cell phone but not to call for help. I suppose when you came out of your blackout, you conversed with your parents about how your day was possibly having a drink of water. What a Hallmark card that was. The only number your family should taught you was 911.

1:00: When we were watching Mariah breathe with mechanical assistance, seeing the pain of loss in Jenna's eyes.

1:30: When we were participating in the sacrament of Extreme Unction Last Rites in a sterile waiting room. We then called family members across America, while you were patiently waiting for the compound to rewrite history. We then began to travel to St. Patrick's Hospital in Missoula.

3:50: When we arrived at St. Pat's, and 15 seconds later were told Mariah would not make it; when we heard our cries, our yells of anger and disbelief bounce off the quiet and somber halls.

4:30: When I did not recognize my baby girl on a gurney being rolled down the hallway. Your daddy had probably called the compound's counsel by this time.

5:30: When I was holding Mariah's lifeless hand, wondering why it all happened.

6:00: When I was watching her cousins walk in and stand still as they looked at Mariah. I was feeling the bile of anger rise because cousin Jessica will never, ever, have her best friend waiting for her in Butte.

6:30: When I turned my cell phone off because too many callers were expressing rage; my own silent rage at knowing Mariah's grandfather and grandmother, Ed and Patty Rademacher, will never have her and Jenna over for their favorite dinner. Knowing her Uncle Tim will never get to tease her.

7:30: When I was wiping Mariah's scrapes and open sores with soft cloths; and hearing the cranium stapler shatter Mariah's skull in an attempt to lessen the hole your grill put in her head; and thinking all I wanted is to grow old with her and watch her and Jenna make my dreams come true. You were probably just snoring in the drunk cell at the jail.

8:30: When I wondered why you felt you had more rights than these girls, the right to drive drunk.

9:30: When I wandered the morning halls of St. Pat's trying to find the answer to the question of Why. And how to explain this ugly event to Mariah's fab five and other friends, while I tried to conjure up some strength to help them. You were probably up, waiting for your mommy and daddy, wondering how they were going to get you out of the criminal deer hit-and-run, and where you were going to eat for breakfast.

11:00: When I was getting briefed on the procedure of relinquishing parental rights over my 14-year-old Mariah's body, so in death she could become an organ donor. Later, we signed the Life Center document. After signing it, we had no say over Mariah, her life, her future. The McCarthys, Rademachers, and Bennies were sitting together but alone in grief in the small hospital room. By this time, you were probably getting bonded out by the compound leader, getting ready to go home.

NOON: When my family hadn't slept or left Mariah for 12 hours. You probably had already gotten home and had a compound-cooked meal, and stretched out and hung with your family, and called your buddies.

1:00 p.m.: When Jenna's friends and many others were traveling to Missoula to say goodbye to her little sister and best friend. You were probably cleaning out your guns. Did you black out at any time? Your friends probably started the thread on Butte Rats to try to blame the girls and the parents to deflect any responsibility on you. I can only guess what some of your good close friends were doing for you.

3:00: When we watched and heard the fine people from the Life Center calling hospitals and emailing others over possible matches. (Ever watch *Grey's Anatomy*

One October Night

in jail the last couple of weeks? Not even close.) By now, you were probably worried about your CDs and other items being stolen from your bully buggy wagon while in the holding yard. I have heard you were more concerned about theft from your weapon of four wheels than the condition of the three girls.

4:00: When we were completing the arrangements for having Mariah's ashes delivered once the organ matches were made. You were probably getting ready to have dinner at the compound. From the looks of you then and now it appears your emotional state and this whole episode hasn't affected your diet or eating regimen before incarceration. I hope you didn't choke on any food while trying to remember the situation or black out during your coming-home dinner party.

5:00: More calls, more visits, more blood transfusions for Mariah to sustain her organs.

8:00: Confirmation of possible donor matches. You were probably getting ready for bed. You had a long day. Having to be enabled to start the denial act and to be coddled from responsibility takes a lot out of a guy like you.

10:00: When we were starting to pack up our belongings for the long ride home of uncertainty and finality. You were probably snoring and daddy was getting the checkbook out.

11:45: When I was singing an Irish lullaby into Mariah's asphalt-scarred ear for the last time. I sang the song into my girls' ears after each was born in the St. James delivery room. I never thought it would be a farewell lullaby.

11:52: When I held back tears while Jenna said goodbye and kissed Mariah on her forehead for the last time. I was screaming silently inside as Janice slowly brushed Mariah's hair from her forehead and kissed her red swollen cheek, then finally released her lifeless hand from her grasp for the last time.

MONDAY, OCTOBER 29, 2007

12:20 A.M.: When we were thanking all of the ICU nurses at St. Pat's. We knew Mariah's organs were being designated for other people so they could live.

2:30: When I stopped by the site and saw the candles and signs. I noticed a light on at the compound, and thought they must be burning the midnight oil while working on discrediting the three girls by placing the blame on everyone, especially the officers and detectives—everyone else except the prince of the compound who was snug and sleeping in his bed dreaming of deer hunting or whatever killers dream of.

3:30: When I looked into my lifeless teenager's room that will never be used by her again, as I heard muffled cries and faint sobbing through shut doors. Before turning off the last remaining light in the house, what did I see but the moonlit compound from my dining room window.

4:30: The first night of forever without Mariah.

If you were anybody else and came from anywhere else than the compound, I would say you owe Jimm, Peggy, Chad, Margi, Mariah, Kaitlyn, Valarie, Janice, and Jenna to live a good life. A life of respect for life—a life of goodness to replace the good gal you killed—and a life of remorse. You owe my wife and my daughter Jenna a future time and place honesty. If you are honored to have children, you need to tell your children the real story of October 27, 2007. You need to show your girls my Mariah's sacred blood print on the walking path, and you owe me to make sure they are aware of your ugliness and evil acts. You owe Mariah to be good.

Alas, though, it's you, and you are from the compound, so it will never happen. The normalcy of the unthinkable is your constitution.

You will be coddled by the system because you were not caught before this time. It takes 250 times for one person to get caught drinking and driving. Knowing the amount of beer you drank makes me believe this isn't the first time you showed sick bravado and drove home drunk. You were conditioned to do this ugly act from past experience. You have done it before and have probably driven from the West Side many times before you made Blacktail Lane a killing field.

The last beer you drank was the blood of Mariah.

This is Mariah's death certificate. Your signature should be beneath the coroner's. This belongs in a frame, hung on a wall in your pen at the compound.

Janice and I, through the help of God, made this. [Mariah's photo.]

You made this. [Photo of Mariah on a gurney.] This is the only picture you and the compound should be allowed to see. I hope this is the last mental image you have as you rest your head on your pillow at night. This is the creation you made that your parents tried so hard to disprove.

When you cry in your cell and as you stifle your moans and shake in anger and are in fear, and you wonder what might come tomorrow, know that you haven't even scratched the surface of our pain and hurt.

Forgiveness is given when asked, forgiveness is given when the asking is genuine, forgiveness will happen to heal those who have been wronged. Forgiveness is forgetting, forgetting is letting go, and sometimes the one asking will never know if they are forgiven. You will be forgiven for our reasons of health and mind, not because you have asked for it. You will be forgiven for our health, not for yours. You will never know when we do.

I fear you will be treated lightly. More compassion than you gave Mariah when you walked over her body, heard her gasp for air, and checked out Valarie and Kaitlyn and heard their pleas for help. You will not be treated by the legal system as you, your family, and your counsel have treated us. We have always been held to a higher standard than the compound. You will not be the victim. You will be coddled by the legal system.

We, the true victims, continue to be the victims by heartless acts and comments from you, your parents, your siblings, and your counsel. And especially by the plea agreement we did not want or support. The whole irony of this ugly experience is that my daughter is killed and I get hate mail. You can tell your buddy, whose victim-blaming and -shaming letter didn't work, I do enjoy my coffee and will enjoy it more knowing you are far away from Jenna, Val, and Kaitlyn.

You, your family, and your counsel have no right to ever criticize me, my family, or the Kilmers or Okrusches, or to judge our actions, or comment on our means. You put us here, you took the blood of my blood away, forever. Try to live, wear our shoes, breathe our air, try to dream of a nightmare. You will not ever be close.

I hold you personally responsible for the death of my daughter, the pain to my family, the injury to her beautiful friends, and the assault on innocence and injury to a whole generation of Butte's youth. If you are to be remembered, I hope it is as a symbol of what not to be and not what to do. What you are needs to be stopped, needs to be used as a guideline of past behavior corrected with responsibility and honesty. It is not normal or the way good people act as youth or as parents.

You will continue to be remembered in your infamy, as will the compound, as more people hear of Mariah and her two friends. This time, nothing will be left out. Count on it, not just in Montana but anywhere good people stand up and say enough is enough, drinking and driving is attempted murder and there is no excuse. When you kill driving drunk, it is murder to me.

The legal system that treats the first DUI as a head cold with a minor fine and some loss of privilege, the legal system that treats the second DUI as a chest cold, with prescribed higher fines, the system that treats the third DUI as a bad case of pneumonia with RX of even higher fines, and the fourth DUI as cancer leading to treatment—that system must change.

I hope it doesn't take more young men like the one who stands convicted before you to make DUI fatalities a serious situation in Butte and Montana, and to make families like the Kilmers, the Okrusches and the McCarthys fodder for a failed system. DUIs are murder waiting to happen.

For everyone in this courtroom, please know that the only thing on the street between someone just like him and you is the double yellow line. This can happen again. [Here I played a recording sent from Mariah's phone.]

Judge Newman, if we do not make a stand and treat this case as a tip of the iceberg and make changes that reflect the seriousness of the crime, then more of our youth will continue to be plowed under by those who scurry and hide and use his actions as a boilerplate way to act once caught. My definition of the banality of evil is that it seems to be okay to disrespect life and normalize the act of not helping those who you hurt and kill. This must be stopped.

We need to show this town that the behavior of drinking and driving, running away and not helping, must stop, that those who do so will be treated harshly both for the underlying crime and for neglecting to aid the injured. Make an example, protect the youth and the law-abiding citizens of Butte. You have heard and listened to our pain. Please use it as guide so others don't have to go through what we did, and so people will know what will happen if they do what he has done.

The targets on the backs of our youth while they are walking will not go away as long as the alcohol-filled hunting scopes are used by him and others while driving their loaded weapons. I have one remaining daughter, our only chance of generational immortality. I don't want her or any more like her killed and to have their deaths rationalized away.

Enough is enough, we need to lock Heaven's gate here from earth by stopping the compound-enabled young men out there from making more memorial sites. Normalizing the unthinkable is no defense, no code of moral conduct.

Butte's youth are our common shared nobility. Protect the real princes and princesses. Not him.

Honor these three beautiful injured princesses, Val, Kaitlyn, and Jenna. They and their generation have lost their innocence. Make what is just right.

Make good out of all this bad.

Honor our dead princess who is forever 14.

Make sure this young man and others like him out there think twice before starting the car and locking one in the chamber.

Our fatality, our finality, should not have happened. Please make Butte safe for the future, so if it does happen again the real victims have some type of justice in this legal system.

Thank you.

Excerpts from

MARIAH'S CHALLENGE

The Story of a Community's Triumph over Tragedy
a drama in one act
by Linda Seeley Piccolo

This play grew out of a year of attendance at court hearings and numerous interviews. It premiered March 18 and 19, 2010, at Jefferson High School in Boulder, Montana. There were seven more performances at high schools across the state. A final performance before a sold-out house of 255 at the Myrna Loy Center in Helena was introduced by Attorney General Steve Bullock. Leo and Jimm also spoke.

Mariah's Challenge was honored by the State Attorney General and the Superintendent of Schools. Much of the dialogue comes directly from those most impacted by this tragedy. Every word spoken by the character of Mariah is from her writing and journals.

Original Cast:

Leo McCarthy: Steven Erickson
Janice McCarthy: Casey Hoffman
Jenna McCarthy: Kaela Williams
Valarie Kilmer: Reba Wacker
Kaitlyn Okrusch: Chelsea Bryant
Chad Okrusch: Jessie Bryant
Margi Okrusch: Robin Dahl
Jimm Kilmer: Brian Warren
Peggy Kilmer: Marqui Hicks
Judge Newman: Daphne Weber
District Attorney: Colin Delli Bovi
Shane Ford: Tyler Brisbee
Doreena Ford: Lindsey Horning
Mariah McCarthy (the voice of): Mikel Overturf

For the full script of this six-scene, fifty-minute play, please contact the author at lindapiccolo@yahoo.com. *Mariah's Challenge* may be performed at no fee with the permission of the playwright. All profits must be used toward events or organizations that sponsor tougher DUI legislation.

Below are generous excerpts from the play. Though they are sequential, they lack the scaffolding of the dramatic structure the full script provides. Excerpts have been selected with a special emphasis on the voices of Mariah, Valarie, and Kaitlyn, and their family members, along with those of Shane Ford, the District Attorney, and the Judge.

With one exception, Leo McCarthy's speeches largely overlap the foregoing narrative, and for that reason are omitted here.

* * *

MARIAH (VOICE-OVER)

On March 12, 1993 a beautiful, cute, lovable Irish girl was born. That's me, Mariah Daye McCarthy. I was born into a loving family of my parents Leo and Janice and my big sister Jenna. She always wanted a sister and when I was little she used to squeeze me so tight I couldn't breathe. She is probably the biggest influence in my life. She is seventeen and a junior in high school. She is pretty and smart and popular. We were more than sisters when we were younger; we were best friends. Now we get along most of the time, but other times she is a huge pain!

I am a typical teenager. I love to play sports and my favorites are volleyball and bowling. I started bowling in the fourth grade and my team was called the Purple Puppies! The next year we became a lot better and I came up with the name the Strike Sisters. We had pink shirts with black trim and our name in cursive on the left side. I took second place in state singles. I still have that trophy. I am really looking forward to my first year in high school and how my life will change.

LEO

Mariah was a good soul. She liked harmony, not drama, laughter not fighting. She loved bowling, watching football, her Irish heritage, popcorn, volleyball, slumber parties, jumping on the trampoline, Christmas morning snowball fights, drive-in movies, her family and her friends. She was a dreamer and she never gave up. Mariah had faith, faith in her sister, faith in her parents, faith in her friends and faith in the hope that good always comes out of bad.

JANICE

Mariah was an old soul with a young heart. She was a dreamer and a thinker, a writer and a memory keeper. She was a collector of treasures, tiny keepsakes, and mementos. She kept notebooks and sketch pads as journals and made lists and planned elaborate birthday parties for her friends. She cherished her family, her friends, and her memories. She greeted each new day with a joyful heart and a spirit of discovery.

* * *

MARIAH (VOICE-OVER)

My best friends and I love to laugh and do the weirdest things together! All we do is laugh, laugh and laugh some more. Sometimes we get into sleeping bags and sumo wrestle on the trampoline. It is so much fun; we call it Mexican Jumping Bean Extravaganza. We videotaped it and everything! We always have fun when we are together.

* * *

MARIAH (VOICE-OVER)

It was the beginning of the school year and we were freshmen in high school. We didn't go with the flow; we stuck up for one another. We didn't care how tall or muscular you were, if you were messing with one of our friends we went crazy. We were great friends, we didn't follow the crowd; we made our own crowd. We laughed and giggled and got silly, but we really cared about each other. Some girls came and went but the true girls stuck till the end.

* * *

VALARIE KILMER

It was the best day. As we were walking we started laughing and talking about friends and our first year in high school. Suddenly Mariah just took off sprinting full speed ahead. She slipped and fell and lay there, on the walking path, laughing hysterically.

KAITLYN OKRUSCH

Then we started skipping, that really brought on the giggles. It was so quiet that our laughter echoed in the darkness.

VALARIE

At one point Mariah slowed down and had to run to catch up. She came barreling and laughing into the middle of the two of us as we continued home.

KAITLYN

It was cold out, but a beautiful, still night. There was a full moon and the ground sparkled with a light dusting of snow. It was magical. We were arm in arm walking down the footpath.

VALARIE

It was almost midnight and the road was empty. It was like we were the only three people awake that night in the whole city.

* * *

SHANE FORD

There are a lot of reasons I shouldn't have been there that night. I was home, getting ready for bed when the night guy called and said some kids had been driving across the new grass at work. I got up, changed, and went down there. I visited with the night guys and decided to buy them pizza. When I got back outside I found out I had locked my keys in the office! So I ran home, got my wife's car, picked up the pizza, and dropped it off with the guys.

On my way back to the house I took Blacktail Lane and I turned up into my street when I see this car facing the wrong way, stopped near a new house under construction. I stopped and started to get out, you know, to see if there was a problem. I see a kid standing by the fence surrounding the construction site and he's looking over it. I'm wondering why, so I start over to him. At this point his truck is blocking my view of the girls. He's in the southbound lane facing north.

He sees me and does a beeline directly to me, very fast, very deliberate. "What happened?" I said. "I hit a deer" he says. Well, he seemed okay, but then he starts to weave backwards and slowly forwards like he's correcting himself. But he has no slurred speech or anything. "Have you been drinking?" I said. He answers: "I had a few."

"Well, your car is in the wrong lane and I can see another car coming down the road now, see their lights? You had better go home."

He walks away and goes for his car and I am in my car and about to drive home when it strikes me funny that I can't see the deer. I think, maybe the deer isn't dead or it's sticking out into the road and could cause another accident, you know? But I can see something, so I back my car up and get out expecting to find a dead animal.

I saw all three of them at once, lying there. My heart just fell out of my chest. I hadn't been there in time to actually see him hit the girls so I didn't know if he had injured them somewhere else and was dumping them here, or what. But then I started finding pieces of his truck and could put two and two together pretty quickly. I knew I couldn't help all three so I ran to the neighbor for help. They come running over with blankets and start warming up the girls. I am standing there, on the side of the road calling 911 when I see the same guy get into his truck, drive north, then back around, make a U-turn and come right at me! I had to jump to avoid being hit!

I am still on the phone to 911, so I tell them he is now heading south. I hang up and run to the girls. Two were moaning and moving a little, but one wasn't moving at all. I went over to her and felt for a pulse. Nothing. So I listened to her breathing. I can't hear anything. So I lean over and say, "You need to help me here. You need to breathe for me." And she does! But then she stops again. I started artificial respiration and I hear her take this huge intake of air. I keep this up until the paramedics arrive to take over. It seems like forever when you're doing that, you know? I really felt she'd be fine once the hospital started working on her. I had every hope for Mariah, she took air very easily.

I don't care how much you've had to drink, you always know if you've hurt someone. You can always call 911 and get help. He wasted a lot of precious time; if he had only yelled for help or said to me "I hurt someone, call 911," people would have forgiven him. But no, he turns around, gets out of his car and stands over them contemplating what to do next.

I mean, here's this guy standing over three broken bodies. It's 22 degrees out and he's doing nothing! They would all have died out there. People make mistakes but no matter how bad they are you got to help them, not leave them like roadkill.

DOREENA FORD

I was home, in my pajamas, waiting for Shane to return when the phone rings and it is our sixteen-year-old son, Zack. He had actually driven by the crash site and saw my car and his dad crouching on the side of the road. He called me and said, "Dad is okay, but I don't think the girls are." I couldn't tell if Shane had been in an accident, or what was going on. I grabbed my coat and I took off down there.

One October Night

When I got there I found Shane kneeling next to Mariah as the EMTs worked on her. Zack was with Kaitlyn Okrusch, lying there, in the snow, talking and joking with her even though she was barely conscious. I stayed with the two girls, holding their hands, talking to them until they were loaded onto stretchers and taken off in the ambulance.

SHANE

I gave my story to the cops and was about to drive home when I changed my mind and decided to try to find the truck and that driver.

Well you can't just go home after a thing like that, and I knew he couldn't be far. Doreena and I took off driving down Blacktail when I see this dirt driveway and the lights of a police car heading down it. I pull up to the house and I see the truck and a policeman leading the kid out of his house. He was easy to recognize, clearly the same guy, and his truck had three dents in the front. The kid is telling the policeman he hadn't driven down Blacktail!

"You're a liar! I saw you. You know you hit those kids!"

DOREENA

I was still in the car. I had the windows rolled down so I could hear what was going on, but this kid scared me; I wasn't getting out. I punched 911 and had my cell phone ready to press "send" if I had to. The policeman said something like, "Is this your truck? Can I look inside?"

SHANE

He kind of freaked and looked right at me, my wife, and the cop, and says "I have a 30-06 in the truck with one in the barrel and two in the magazine." What was that about? Was he actually threatening to kill the three of us? Shortly afterwards another two police cars pull up and we can finally go home.

DOREENA

The police said he had made eleven cell phone calls in the seventeen minutes after the crash and none of them were to 911! What kind of person could do that?

SHANE

His name was [redacted]. He was nineteen years old and had twenty-four beers that night before he drove home. He had no intention of admitting responsibility.

He hit those babies, pulled into the street, turned around, pulled over, and walked around them as they lay on the ground bleeding. I don't know where you come down on the idea of a higher power, but I believe God wanted me there that night. Whatever he had planned to do, I truly believe God put me there so he didn't do something worse.

* * *

MARIAH (VOICE-OVER)

I love art and won two contests. In the fourth grade I won the Energy Share Contest and in the fifth I won the Christmas Stroll Button Design! I am a writer and a poet and I am very happy with who I am. I am a dreamer and I don't give up easily.

* * *

JENNA

That night I went to a late night movie with friends. On my way home I saw a truck with its passenger headlight burned or cracked out. I didn't think anything of it and headed on home. Never did I think I would be staring at the driver of that same truck in a courtroom, staring at the man who killed my little sister.

* * *

MARGI OKRUSCH

Chad and I were home when we got the call saying the girls had been hit by a car and to come right to the hospital. We were terrified and confused. I grabbed the two kids and rushed to the ER. We didn't say anything on the way up there, I just cried and prayed. I had no idea what to expect. When they took us into the ER, our worst nightmare came true.

PEGGY KILMER

I had just returned home from the theatre when I get a phone call from a woman who asks, "Are you Val's mom?" She says there's been an accident, it's not good and to come right away. At first I can't believe it. I had just spoken to Valarie not twenty minutes earlier. They were at Mariah's house for a slumber party. How could they possibly have been in an accident?

When Jimm and I arrived all three of the girls were still lying on the ground. We ran to Valarie who could speak, but was falling in and out of consciousness. She was very scared, very confused, and every movement was agony for her. They put

Valarie and Mariah next to each other in the emergency room, with just the panel separating the two areas. Kaitlyn was in a room around the corner. We were all so close I could hear every cry, moan and whimper.

MARGI

Even now I can't think about that night; it's like a nightmare that I can't wake up from. We kept pacing, crying, waiting to hear back on all the tests and scans. Hoping and praying, making deals with God for our daughter's life.

PEGGY

We stayed with Valarie all night sitting next to her bed, touching her hand as machines pumped blood and fluids into her tiny arms. It was impossible to sleep. All I could do was pray and wonder whether she'd be alright, need surgery, survive.

* * *

PEGGY

I stayed in the room with Valarie. She was able to see Kaitlyn just before she went home, but she didn't ask about Mariah after that first night. I know now she didn't have the strength to hear the answer. She found that strength at four on Thursday morning.

* * *

JANICE

It was all like a video or a bad movie, playing over and over again, that I was unable to turn off. When I look back on Mariah's life, I think now that she wasn't destined to be with us long. As a child she was always looking up at the sky, at the clouds. She loved pictures of angels and drew them, even from an early age. When she was seven her Grandpa died. Mariah used to write him letters in heaven and draw pictures of him as an angel. Years ago I had given her a clip-on angel which she kept on her pillow, year after year, even when the wings fell off. It is still there today.

* * *

DISTRICT ATTORNEY

Ten years ago if I asked for a verdict of negligent homicide in a case such as this I would have been considered a zealot and an overreaching prosecutor and laughed out of the courtroom. Two years ago there were no criminal charges for a hit and run resulting in death in this state. We have come a long way since then, but not long enough. These victims and their families should not have to stand in court asking you to send a killer to prison. By driving drunk, [he] took away the innocence of our entire community. He made us all afraid to let our children play outside or walk home from school. He put targets on our backs and made us all prisoners in our own town, fearful of the next drunk driver that comes along. We can stop that today. We have come a long way from the days of allowing drunk drivers to rule our streets. Those days are done. They are over. Let's stand up for our rights as citizens to be safe on our sidewalks and streets. If we don't take a stand, here, today, then the only thing separating each of us from another drunk driver is a six inch wide white line.

JUDGE NEWMAN

Before I impose sentence the victims and their families would like to address the court. The court calls Margi Okrusch, mother of Kaitlyn.

MARGI

I am not here because I am perfect. I am not perfect and I am not judging you. You had four opportunities to change the outcome of that night. You stopped your car, but when given the chance to offer assistance to our three girls, you chose instead to run away. Instead of calling 911, you got in your truck and drove home, leaving them there to die in the cold. Instead of asking Shane Ford to get help, you attempted to cover up your crime. Instead of behaving like an adult and taking responsibility for your actions, you behaved like a selfish child and left your mess for others. You caused unimaginable pain and grief for all of us. You need to step up to the light. You need to face what you've done and accept responsibility. You need to stand up and be a man. It's not too late.

JUDGE NEWMAN

Next to address the court will be Chad Okrusch, father of Kaitlyn.

CHAD OKRUSCH

On the night of October 27, my daughter Kaitlyn was fourteen years old. She was an active, happy, and healthy teenager. Your callous and reprehensible actions left her moaning and struggling for her life on a dark street in freezing temperatures. She had facial lacerations, deep cuts to her left foot and right calf, multiple bruises, and a subarachnoid hemorrhage in her skull.

One October Night

You caused these injuries, but instead of taking responsibility for your actions you drove away leaving three little girls to die in the street like roadkill. People tell me again and again this is a tragedy for all concerned. I prayed for you that night in the hospital while I was praying that my daughter and her friends would live to walk out with us. But I became more and more angry as the details of the wreck came to light. In part you are a victim of our culture and our world, a world that turns a blind eye to underage drinking; but when you do something wrong you need to pay. There is a long road between law and justice. You are stepping onto that road today. It is up to you which direction you take.

JUDGE NEWMAN

Kaitlyn Okrusch will now speak.

KAITLYN

Do I look like a deer to you? I am wondering what I can do to try to relieve my pain. You have made my life a living hell. Not just for me, but for all of us and for this community. What is wrong with you? I feel terribly sorry for you. I have dreams and hopes. I wonder if you will ever look inside yourself and see that you have no self-respect. You have lost nothing but we have lost everything. We lost Mariah. I wish you could have met her. She was really special, you know? You may have broken me physically but you have not destroyed me. Something beautiful has risen out of your negligence, love. Love keeps each of us going, our love of Mariah, our love of each other, love of doing right, and the knowledge that Mariah is still with us. She is an angel watching over us. Turn to Mariah; she is the one you need to apologize to. She is the one who will set you free.

JUDGE NEWMAN

Next to speak will be Jimm Kilmer, father of Valarie.

JIMM KILMER

Since that night we have all been in a state of sustained trauma. You have made us victims of your shameful and deceitful actions. I won't expose the extent it has affected Valarie. You have taken so much from us and from this community. I will tell you you are responsible, whether you accept the responsibility or not, for changing Valarie into the person you see today. You robbed her of the joy a teenager should feel. For Valarie, every normal happy event that a teenager should be enjoying collides with unbearable grief. October 27 was her last happy day. As you drove away she lay on the roadside with a subarachnoid hemorrhage, a lacerated liver, kidney, and spleen, a spot on her brain, lower back vertebrae shift, multiple bruises, and an elbow cut open to the bone. The memory of that night will haunt all of us forever. Valarie was in and out of consciousness, yet she begged her mother to find Mariah and Kaitlyn, putting her own fear aside thinking only of her friends. You struck her so hard she was knocked out of her shoes and left lying on a cold roadside for forty-four minutes in shock and trauma, and yet, she thought only of them.

We all carry unbearable pain. I think of standing in the emergency room with parents whose kids mean everything to them, desperately hoping their girls will be alright. Then to see those same parents when they learn one of them will not survive. You have taken so much from us; from all of us, especially the McCarthy family. Do you have the courage to look in the face of Mariah's parents, her heartbroken sister, her grandparents? Only God will ever know the depths of their sorrow.

When I look at you I tremble. What were you going to do with our three girls if Shane Ford hadn't intervened? Decent people don't behave like this. You have built a prison for yourself with lies, when only the truth will set you free. Show some maturity and compassion. Apologize, take responsibility for your actions. They were three kids walking down the street on their way home. Honor them. Honor Mariah. Honor every victim of a drunk driver in this country and turn your life around for all of them.

Judge Newman, please don't make this a case of making victims out of victims. Please make our community a place where all can be safe and violators will be punished. Let this be the turning point in a community that takes care of each other. How many of our children must die before we say enough is enough? Help us change our society and create a cultural environment where drinking and driving are never condoned.

[Leo McCarthy's speech is omitted.]

JUDGE NEWMAN

I am certain there is nothing I can do today to satisfy everyone concerned. I cannot turn back the clock to October 27. I cannot undo what you did. I cannot give back the McCarthy's daughter. Should I order him locked up? Should we throw away the key? Should I return him to the community? The truth lies somewhere in the middle.

There is no evidence of intention to commit harm. But death and injury resulted from a series of choices you made. You chose to drink. You chose to drive. You chose to disregard the risk to life and community. You chose to flee from the scene. You had the opportunity to do what was right. You didn't seize it. You neither called for nor offered assistance to your victims. The court must take all this into consideration when passing sentence.

And yet, you are young with no prior criminal record. You may still return and eventually become a productive member of the community. Take the memory of October 27 and use it to create something good. Serve this community and state. I look forward to that day.

I therefore sentence you to ten years in the state prison for negligent vehicular homicide. You are also sentenced to ten years, suspended, on two counts of negligent vehicular assault and hit and run driving involving death and personal injury. You will begin serving this sentence immediately.

* * *

JANICE

At first I tried to just get through each day after Mariah's death, but it was all a fog. Everything was spinning; I couldn't breathe. The sun came up and the sun went down, but anything in between I couldn't say.

Now, a year later, I try to remember her as she was before the crash. I remember who she was and what she brought to all of us in her little life. I exist in an artificial prison where no sunlight ever enters. I live with a dull hard ache. I can't let grief define me. I've lived in grief; it's not a pretty place. It drains you mentally and physically. Now I acknowledge the past and realize I can't predict the future, but I have to live in the present. I have to remember what she was, not the crash scene. Honestly, I'd rather be gone from this earth, but I still have Jenna and I know life must go on.

One of my greatest memories is that night, the night she died, when she stood at the door to say goodbye. She was giggling and laughing when I agreed to let the three of them walk the boys home. She grabbed her coat and turned to me with that big smile and said, "Thanks, Mom." I freeze that picture in my mind.

JENNA

Mariah may not be here physically, but now she exists in other ways, I can feel it. She is my angel. I'll always miss her and I'll never forget her, because I love her; all that she was; all that she is. My life has been worse than I ever imagined it would be, but I guess that's life and you have to go on living it no matter what happens because you are still alive. The pain I feel is part of life. The confusion and fear I feel are there to remind me that somewhere out there is something better than this life, and that is something worth fighting for. Someday I'll wake up and realize that all the pain I've felt in my life will have been worth it because at that point my life will be exactly what I've always wanted.

JANICE

Mariah had cleaned and redecorated her bedroom just before she died. She put her Grandpa's picture on her desk and her angel book by her bed. I like to sit there, remembering her. Lately I've been finding journals, poems, pieces of paper she's drawn or written on. Just when I think I've found them all, another turns miraculously up. That is her gift to me. That is how I know she will always be with me.

When my girls were little I told them feathers were a sign that angels had been around them. Since that night we've all been finding them, especially Jenna.

JENNA

Feathers are everywhere. I've found them inside school, inside my house, and inside my laundry. I found a tiny little one on my left wrist just this morning while I was washing my face.
Signs like that help me know that Mariah is in a good, safe place.

VALARIE

Feathers? Yes, I've found them too. One day, shortly after I came back to school, I was walking down the hallway and came to a spot where Mariah and I used to meet between classes. There, where we used to stand was this big, colorful feather, right there. I know Mariah is with us, with me, always.

JENNA

Every night when my family eats dinner, I set the table. I always have and I always will. The reality of Mariah's death really hit me when I was setting the table for dinner and she wasn't there. I realized at that moment that I had to only take out three plates, three forks, three knives, three spoons, and three glasses. I don't like three; I like four. I don't think I will ever get used to three.

KAITLYN

I still wonder, "Why Mariah, why not me?" I am thankful to be alive but the guilt that comes with life is almost unbearable. Mariah was the strongest of us. I believe God chose Mariah and the McCarthy family because they are all so strong. God chooses the strong to make everyone else stronger. I know Mariah is guiding us all the time.

MARGI

We have all lived with the guilt. He hit three girls. Why did one die and two survive? Why Mariah and not Kaitlyn or Valarie? We will never know the how or why. Every day I think of Janice, Leo, and Jenna. I look at Kaitlyn and I cannot imagine my life without her or what the McCarthys have gone through, are still going through. Every day I tell Kaitlyn how much I love her and remember how lucky I am to have her with us.

VALARIE

Now, I accept that I can't change that night, but I can't allow it to change me. After the crash I was afraid to go to school or to walk outside. I still have bad days, but they are fewer and fewer. I miss her terribly. All we have are the memories of her in our hearts.

PEGGY

Everything is bittersweet. I am so grateful to see Valarie laugh and smile again, but there isn't a day that goes by that I don't think about the McCarthy family. They call it survivor's guilt. We have all asked ourselves that question and will probably continue to ask it. I know we won't get the answer here on this earth, and Valarie knows it as well. But she and Kaitlyn have a beautiful faith in their church and know they will see her again.

* * *

MARIAH (VOICE-OVER)

Butte, Montana, is the only place where I can imagine growing up. New York, San Diego, or Miami just wouldn't feel right. A little town known for tough kids and no civilization is the one place I feel like I belong. The protective mountains are barriers against natural disasters and they make me feel safe. In this goofy little town everyone knows everyone. No, we aren't hillbillies; we are just friendlier than your average Americans town.

* * *

VALARIE

I am part of the Challenge. It's my way to keep Mariah alive. I always want to keep her in my life and in everything I do.

KAITLYN

The Challenge is a big part of my life but it hurts when others just give up. After the crash everyone was committed to supporting the Challenge and taking a vow not to drink. But after a few months they fell away. It's hard to change something that's gone on for so long, hard to change people's perceptions and habits.

JENNA

Exactly, I am in a glass social bubble. People don't talk about anything that has to do with partying around me. I guess I appreciate that. Sometimes people stare at me because I am the "dead girl's sister." When I came back to school after it happened everyone was nice to me. I had lots of friends for a while, and no one was ever going to drink again. But things gradually got back to normal and those who partied before are probably still doing it. I wonder if we can ever get through to them unless someone they love dies from a drunk driver.

KAITLYN

Val and I don't fit in anymore. I guess it's hard to be the kid who doesn't drink when those around you do. Teenagers just don't want to be the odd one out.

VALARIE

It's true; we don't get invited places much because they know we won't drink. Then at school on Monday they'll be talking about their weekend and clam up when we walk by. They don't see tomorrow. They can't imagine the consequences of just one mistake.

About the Playwright:

Linda Piccolo taught Theatre at Jefferson High School in Boulder, Montana, for twenty-five years, and was the Montana State Theatre educator of the year in 2013. Her troupe of actors won five state and two national theatre championships. In 1997 they performed at the world's largest theatre festival, the Fringe, in Edinburgh, Scotland. For years she sponsored the Mariah's Challenge Club at Jefferson High. She remains an advocate for strong legislation against drunk and impaired drivers and underage drinking.

Tap 'er Light: The Best We All Can Be

by Bill Foley—Nov 5, 2007, for *The Montana Standard*

Sometimes it takes a tragedy to see the best in people.

Friday night, the Billings Skyview volleyball team beat Butte High in a playoff game in Billings.

During the game, the Skyview players and coaches wore purple ribbons to honor Mariah McCarthy, the 14-year-old Butte girl who died last week from injuries sustained in a hit-and-run accident involving an alleged drunk driver.

I know I'm not the only Butte person now hoping the Falcons win the Class AA state title this weekend in Bozeman. That team has some serious karma on its side.

The Falcons, by the way, are coached by Vicki Carle, the wife of former Butte High basketball star Mike Carle.

I also know I'm not the only one who was moved by McCarthy's father last week.

Hands down, watching Leo McCarthy's speech at his daughter's funeral was the most impressive thing I've ever witnessed, and that includes the Red Sox 2004 comeback from an 0-3 deficit against the Yankees.

Leo fought back his unimaginable sadness and spoke of making something positive out of a horrible situation.

He encouraged the generations of his two daughters to be the first from Butte not to drink.

In a speech John F. Kennedy couldn't have topped, Leo spoke of how he hopes Mariah's message—don't drink and drive—will make him the last member of the "lonely club" no father would ever want to join.

It was heartbreaking to see so many of Mariah's friends—young and old—suffering in unexplainable sorrow, and the funeral crowd was larger than what most Butte basketball games will see this season—a true testament to a great family and a beautiful young lady.

Yet Leo's words somehow seemed to comfort a community that sleepwalked through the last week.

I know I'm not alone in saying it's been so hard to think of anything but the victims and families involved in the awful tragedy. Nothing else seems to matter. Not even the World Series.

Through teary eyes I posted the following on Butterats.com late last Monday night: "Last night I watched the Red Sox win the World Series. It should have been one of the greatest nights of my life because much of my life has revolved around rooting for the team to do just that.

"Yet, as my team was winning on TV I often felt myself fighting back tears because I knew my good friend Leo McCarthy, quite possibly the nicest man in the whole world, had to be going through hell.

"Instead of hooting and hollering about the game, I felt myself hugging and kissing my 4-year-old girl and telling her I love her to the point of bugging her. I have never been so sad for someone as I am for Leo and his family. I can't even begin to fathom the pain they must feel, and I wish there was something we could do for them.

"When something like this happens, there are no words good enough. Walter Payton, one of my biggest heroes, knew when he was dying and wrote an autobiography.

"Here is a line from that book: 'If you love someone, tell him or her, for you never know what tomorrow may have in store. Remember, tomorrow is promised to no one.' "Perhaps the best way we can honor the memory of young Mariah McCarthy is by reminding our loved ones how we feel about them, and treating every day as if it could be the last." Of course there is another obvious way we can honor the victims. It's so simple that it shouldn't even have to be said. Unfortunately it must.

Let's change this culture that accepts drinking and driving as something we all do.

A lot of us have driven drunk. Lots of people reading these words will do it again tonight.

We all have to look in the mirror and tell ourselves that it's time for this crap to stop.

Individually we have to take a stand and hope the younger generations pay attention.

There's no time like the present to one-by-one change this stupid mindset. "Not even once," as the anti-meth ads say, should go for drinking and driving as well. Not even once. Not even one beer.

Next time you've had a few at the bar and are going to drive home, stop for a second. Before you turn the ignition, think one time of Mariah and her two friends—Valarie Kilmer and Kaitlyn Okrusch—who were struck by the same truck.

Then hand the keys to a sober friend, call for a ride or walk home.

You can surely count me in as one of the converted, and I pray that I'm not alone.

Together we can all do our part to let three young Butte girls bring out the best in all of us. ❖

21 Butte Seniors Honored

at 10th Annual Mariah's Challenge Scholarship Ceremony

by Maddie Vincent, May 20, 2019

Last Thursday night, 21 Butte seniors were honored at the 10th annual Mariah's Challenge Scholarship Ceremony for staying dedicated to preventing underage drinking all through high school.

And for Leo McCarthy, founder of Mariah's Challenge and father of Mariah McCarthy, this 10-year milestone of the scholarship program proves to him that Butte can change.

"The tombstone of Mariah is my and my family's constitution to always be there for the youth and to encourage them to take the challenge," McCarthy said. "And the success of the challenge is a testament to Butte's ability to change."

On October 28, 2007, Mariah Daye McCarthy, 14, was hit and killed by a car driven by a 20year-old man while she was walking with her two friends to her house for a sleepover around midnight on a Sunday. The man, Wade Petersen, was under the influence of alcohol when he hit the three teens.

Mariah's friends lived through their injuries, but Mariah died as a result of hers in a Missoula hospital.

Less than a year later, McCarthy started the Mariah Daye McCarthy Scholarship Foundation, better known as Mariah's Challenge, with a three-fold mission: to educate teens about the dangers of drinking; to educate parents about the dangers and signs of teen alcohol abuse; and to foster a cultural change in Butte, a town with a long history of alcohol use and abuse.

"Regardless of how emotional and hard it is for us to do this, the Butte youth is worth it," McCarthy said. "It's always been about the youth and turning a really bad and ugly into a beautiful good."

Teens that accept Mariah's Challenge as a high school student to remain drug and alcohol free can apply for the $1,000 Mariah's Challenge Scholarship the spring of their senior year. The challenge explicitly states: "If you are under 21, do not drink and never get into a car with somebody who has been drinking."

McCarthy then interviews each applicant and chooses who will receive the scholarship award based on a senior's adherence to the challenge, as well as their character and community commitments.

"A lot of them indicated that they understand what the current atmosphere is and that they chose not to fall into it ... they were resilient for themselves, which was really impressive," McCarthy said of this year's awardees.

At last Thursday's scholarship ceremony in the Montana Tech Auditorium, the Class of 2019 Mariah's Challenge Scholarship recipients were honored and celebrated for this resiliency, McCarthy said. Local, state and national leaders like Bob Bennie, co-founder of Mariah's Challenge and Mariah's uncle, Gov. Steve Bullock and Sen. Jon Tester spoke to the 21 seniors via video, and both McCarthy and keynote speaker Rob O'Neill spoke to the awardees in person.

McCarthy said he wanted O'Neill to speak at the ceremony because of his continued interest in Mariah's Challenge and the resiliency he's shown throughout his life. O'Neill was also the primary financial sponsor of the 2019 ceremony.

During O'Neill's speech, he talked about his experience serving in the U.S. Navy, specifically with SEAL Team Six, and the story behind the death of Osama Bin Laden. Through sharing his experiences, O'Neill said he hoped to encourage the award recipients in the room to maintain a positive attitude, block out any negativity and to keep moving forward, no matter what.

"It doesn't matter what you look like or where you're from, you can do anything you want with a positive attitude," O'Neill said to the audience, standing behind a podium on the Tech stage above a banner that read "Have you accepted Mariah's Challenge?"

McCarthy took the stage after O'Neill spoke. He echoed O'Neill's sentiments of maintaining positivity and resilience, but also spoke about how much the seniors' success in completing Mariah's Challenge has impacted him as her father.

"You are Leo's heroes! If someone gives you crap, give them my cell number. You make Butte better!" McCarthy said to the 21 seniors.

"For me, when the shadows of grief get long and suffocating, I look to my family, my friends and I think of a quote I used in Mariah's eulogy… 'Faith is believing when it is beyond the power of reasoning.' Mariah's Challenge is the embodiment of that quote. You to me are the living example of that quote."

The 2019 Mariah's Challenge Scholarship Recipients were: Madison Hash, McKenzie Norton, Hallie Blakeley, Allyson Cleverly, Jaden Cleveland, Justise Birkenbuel, Kerra Luebeck, Alexander Cross, Charles Renouard, Kendall Storer, Kama Muccie, Clayton Heggem, Connor Heggem, Margaret LaFave, Joslyn Klapan, McKenzie Faulkner, Clint Connors, Brittney Tierney, William Cunneen, Seth Gardner, and Bella Sorini. ❖

Thanks & Acknowledgments

I have thanked many in these pages, and will no doubt forget some who deserve to be named. Here, let me again thank Janice and Jenna, and my clan on both sides, and also acknowledge the contributions of the following good souls:

Dillon, Montana, Agent Ted Ori for mustering a sizable donation from Montana State Farm Agents to start a fledgling plea for change.

Butte physician Mike Gallagher and his family for generous support at the outset.

Mike Bauer for his unselfish acts in the form of ten innovative basketball tournaments called the Crossroads Shootout.

Keith Sayers for building a metal cross with iron donated from Pacific Steel and Recycling. It has MARIAH carved into the horizontal section. At the bottom of the cross is a light mechanism to display her name shadowed in red. The cross was erected where Mariah moved on and her body came to rest after the collision.

Travis Hettick for his annual mobilization of full-contact football games called the Pig Bowl.

All who have played in our much less strenuous annual golf tournament.

All who have helped through sidewalk sales, Kool-Aid stands, and memorials for lost loved ones.

Jon Wick, past CEO of Mariah's Challenge and diligent author, producer, and distributor of Mariah's Messenger, and originator of Light Up Mariah.

Ron Davis, early promoter and steady PSA at his radio station.

Paul Panisko for his comedic personality that makes each scholarship event memorable.

John Emiegh for his reporting and for giving an introduction to the Challenge, and for adding substance via newspaper and TV.

The past and current board members of the 501(c)(3).

Jimm Kilmer, father of Valarie, for his support and help in presenting at many events in Montana, Nashville, San Mateo, California, and at the CNN Top Ten Show in Los Angeles.

Chad Okrusch, father of Kaitlyn, for all his help and for being a road mate during the early presentations. His song "Angel Mariah" appears on his album *Wisdom Road*. The song, which I first heard soon after the funeral, has stayed with me.

East Middle School for including Mariah's Fun Run, during which they wear varied team colors with the Mariah's Challenge logo, in their Character Counts Week. Bill Bartholomew and Larry Driscoll, both past principals, and current principal Keith Miller have also honored Mariah's Challenge by inviting me on an annual basis to talk to the whole school. Inclusion in their Teens in Partnership (TIP) education program has developed into a tradition and a cooperative adventure.

The BU Bunch, an inspiring group whose philosophy is elegantly stated by its motto: "B-ing who U are." Member Corey Gransbury designed a gorgeous piece of art, an angelic necklace called McCarthy. Formed by Kellie Norman Johnston, Chrissy Vetter, Becky Colvin, Nicole McArthur, Keli Fivey, and Corey, the BU Bunch is a microcosm of all Butte has to offer.

Brian O'Connor, an outstanding educator at Seven Bridges Middle School in Chappaqua, NY, for incorporating the Challenge's tenets and discussing the pitfalls of teenage drinking as part of a yearly program that spotlights a CNN Top Ten Hero. The McCarthy family made a personal visit, which was both humbling and rewarding, and which led to an ongoing friendship with Brian, his wife Tara, daughter Alix, and son James. We continue to participate in annual Skype sessions. Several seniors from Jefferson High School in Boulder, and Whitehall High School, both in Jefferson County, for participating in our annual awards ceremony.

A-1 Ambulance for their care to the three girls, the Butte SilverBow police and detectives and the County Attorneys for their expertise and professionalism, St. James Community Hospital and St Patrick's Hospital in Missoula for their amazing physicians and nurses.

Thank you also to Darrell and Lisa Turley for their kind decoration of the site.

A special thanks to Montana Tech, whose administration and athletic department incorporated Mariah's Challenge as announced acknowledgments at their football, men's and women's basketball, and volleyball games. Amanda Badovinic, in particular, helped us reserve the auditorium and provided refreshments and bakery items.

Thank you to Bill Foley and Jon Wick, who were the genesis of this book

Bob Bennie was a tremendous help in getting Mariah's Challenge off the ground.

Last but not least, thanks to Linda Piccolo, for her insightful play, and for writing the Foreword. And to all the actors, directors, and backstage workers who brought her play to life. ❖

A Prayer in Closing

This book is a personal prayer of gratitude, hope, and love, a nondenominational plea

>for the power of parenting and for making the dinner table the most powerful place in the world

>for cultural and personal renewal and for salvation

>for us to watch the rising generation enjoy life without the callous ripping away of adolescence and innocence through heartless actions

>for underage drinking as a rite of passage to become a thing of the past

>for Mariah's Wish to come true, so that every young person in Butte, Montana, USA, and the world can take Mariah's Challenge and Grow Old, Grow Old with their parents, Grow Old with their kids who have kids of their own.

About the Author

Leo McCarthy was born and raised in Walkerville and Butte, Montana, the youngest of eleven children. He graduated from Montana Western College and held jobs ranging from coaching football to substitute teaching at the high school level to a stint in the rehabilitation field. He then found his career with State Farm Insurance, first as a claims adjuster, and for the last twenty-four years running his own agency. He and his wife Janice (Rademacher) McCarthy were blessed with two gorgeous daughters, Jenna and Mariah. Mariah currently resides in heaven.

In 2008, Leo established the Mariah Daye McCarthy Scholarship Foundation, known as Mariah's Challenge, and with others has spoken to high school students nationwide. In 2009, he represented the Challenge in *People* magazine's MLB All-Stars Among Us, and in 2012 he was selected as a CNN Top Ten Hero.

A Montana Tech booster and member of the Butte Chamber of Commerce, Leo also belongs to many other civic organizations. He is a follower of the Roman Catholic faith, holds a Black Belt in Taekwondo, and is a survivor of marathons in New York and Chicago. Currently, to the limits of his aging body, he enjoys CrossFit. As a reader, Leo is especially drawn to the Roman Stoic philosophers and anything to do with history.

For more information visit mariahschallenge.com.